...ards
Hidden History

Eleanor Ghey

Hoards
Hidden History

The British Museum

© 2015 The Trustees of the
British Museum

Eleanor Ghey has asserted the right to be
identified as the author of this work

First published in 2015 by
The British Museum Press
A division of The British Museum
Company Ltd
38 Russell Square
London WC1B 3QQ
britishmuseum.org

A catalogue record for this book is
available from the British Library

ISBN 978 0 7141 1825 3

Designed by Jade Design
Printed in Italy by Printer Trento S.r.l.

The papers used in this book are
recyclable products made from wood
grown in well-managed forests and other
controlled sources. The manufacturing
processes are expected to conform to the
environmental regulations of the country
of origin.

Frontispiece: A selection of items from the
Staffordshire hoard before cleaning.
Right: Gilded silver pepper pot in the form
of a female bust from the Hoxne hoard.
Height 103 mm.

Contents

Timeline

Beaker period 2500–2000 BC
Amesbury Archer, Wiltshire (2400–2200 BC)

Early Bronze Age 2200–1500 BC

Middle Bronze Age 1500–1100 BC

Towednack hoard, Cornwall (1300–1150 BC)
Beginning of deposits at Flag Fen and Must Farm,
    City of Peterborough
Salcombe wreck, Devon (1300–1150 BC)

Late Bronze Age 1100–800/700 BC

Isleham hoard, Cambridgeshire (1150–1000 BC)
Milton Keynes hoard, Buckinghamshire (1150–800 BC)
Heathery Burn cave site, County Durham (1100-600 BC)
Mooghaun hoard, County Clare, Ireland (1150–750 BC)
Tarves hoard, Aberdeenshire, Scotland (1000–850 BC)
Broadness hoard, River Thames, Kent (1000–750 BC)
Boughton Malherbe hoard, Kent (950–800 BC)
Langton Matravers hoard, Dorset (800–600 BC)

Iron Age 800 BC–AD 43
Roman Republic 509–27 BC

Vale of Wardour hoard, Wiltshire (c. 600 BC)
Batheaston hoard, Bath and North East Somerset
    (c. 450–300 BC)
Chiseldon cauldrons, Wiltshire (c. 400–200 BC)
Salisbury (or Netherhampton) hoard, Wiltshire (c. 200–100 BC)
Snettisham hoards, Norfolk (c. 150–50 BC)
Chute hoard, Wiltshire (80–60 BC)
Westerham hoard, Kent (80–60 BC)
Sedgeford hoard, Norfolk (60–50 BC)
Jersey hoard, Channel Islands (60–50 BC)
Winchester hoard, Hampshire (75–25 BC)
Orton Meadows currency bars, Peterborough (c. 150–50 BC)
Spetisbury Rings currency bars, Dorset (c. 150–50 BC)

Roman Britain AD 43–410
Roman Empire 27 BC–AD 476

Stanwick hoard, North Yorkshire (50 BC–AD 100)
Polden Hill hoard, Somerset and Westhall hoard, Suffolk
    (AD 50–150)
Owermoigne hoard, Dorset (41–54)
Hallaton, Leicestershire (41–54 and earlier)
South Warwickshire hoard, Warwickshire
    (after 63–4)
Ribchester hoard, Lancashire (c. 120)
Corbridge armour, Northumberland (122–38)
Snettisham jeweller's hoard, Norfolk
    (154–61)
Corbridge gold coins, Northumberland (159–60)
Selby area hoard, East Riding of Yorkshire (176–81)
Tadcaster hoard, North Yorkshire (192)
Muswell Hill hoard, Greater London (209–11)
Yeovil hoard, Somerset (269–71)
Beau Street hoard, Bath, Bath and North East Somerset (272–4)
Cunetio hoard, Wiltshire (272–4)
Frome hoard, Somerset (286–93)
Felmingham Hall hoard, Norfolk (c. 100–300)
Barkway hoard, Hertfordshire (c. 200–300)
Ashwell hoard, Hertfordshire (c. 250–400)
Milton Keynes (Fenny Stratford) forger's hoard, Buckinghamshire
    (c. 275–400)
Lincoln hoard, Lincolnshire (327–8)
Shrewsbury hoard, Shropshire (333–5)
Newby hoard, Cumbria (335–40)
Shapwick hoard, Somerset (395–402 or later)
Mildenhall hoard, Suffolk (c. 300–400)
Thetford hoard, Norfolk (390 or later)
Water Newton hoard, Cambridgeshire (c. 300–400)
Hoxne hoard, Suffolk (407–8 or later)
Coleraine hoard, County Londonderry, Northern Ireland
    (407–8 or later)

Anglo-Saxon c. 410–1100
Visigothic Rome c. 410–507
Byzantine Empire 476–1453
Merovingian France c. 457–754

Patching hoard, West Sussex (461–70)
Oxborough hoard, Norfolk (474–5)
St Martin's Cemetery, Canterbury, Kent
  (buried c. 590–630)
Sarre necklace, Kent (c. 615–75)
Sutton Hoo purse, Suffolk (610–35)
Crondall hoard, Hampshire (640)
Staffordshire hoard, near Lichfield, Staffordshire (c. 675–725)
Woodham Walter hoard, Essex (730)
Hurbuck hoard, County Durham (c. 800–1000)

Viking period c. 865–1066

Cuerdale hoard, Lancashire (905–10)
Vale of York hoard, North Yorkshire (c. 927–9)
Penrith (Flusco Pike) hoard, Cumbria (900–50)
Halton Moor hoard, Lancashire (c. 1025)

Medieval period 1066–1500
Norman Conquest 1066

Box hoard, Wiltshire 1142
Colchester hoard I, Essex (1248)
Colchester hoard II, Essex
  (1256 and 1268–78)
Tutbury hoard, Staffordshire (1321)
Fishpool hoard, Nottinghamshire (1463–4)

Post-medieval period after 1500
English Civil War 1642–51

Bitterley hoard, Shropshire (1643)
Breckenbrough hoard, North Yorkshire (1644)
Netherhampton spoons, Wiltshire (after 1632)
Cheapside hoard, City of London (c. 1640–66)

Samuel Pepys buries money (1667)
Chancery hoard, City of London (1690s)

World War II 1939–45

Hackney hoard, Greater London (1913, buried 1940)

BOOTY

ERIC FINDS £10M BOOTY

Digs it up on fa...

news | 13

d of Roman gold glisters once more

Under the 1996 Treasure Act the find was notified to the City ...coroner. It was then...

June, said: "You just do not expect this on an archaeological site. I was merely cleaning an area after removing the...

...lus coins is to go on show in Somerset county museum soon, more than two years after coming to light.
The 9213 third century coins ...discovered by treasure... and

Severn, the archaeologist who unearthed the coins last June, called the discovery the 'find of a lifetime'

Picture: JONATHAN EVANS/RSR

A chance sweep of a farm field unearthed the most important hoard of Roman gold and silver artefacts found in Britain. David...

ALBAN DOHENOE

Left: Eric Lawes, who found the Ro...

...st for far...

12 **NEWS**

Boudic
hoard

The Herts
ADVERTISER
Visit our website at www.hertsad24.co.uk
Proudly serving the communities of St Albans, Radlett, Bricket Wood and surrounding district since 1855

St Albans Edition
June 6, 2013 No. 8355 75p

Treasure hunter's debut detecting session uncovers massive haul of buried Roman coins

Gold finder will never forget the first time

hertsad.co.uk

metal detectorist discovered ...d of Roman gold coins ...UK on his first ever outing ...pest equipment he could ...heard yesterday.
...gon found the ...Sandridge ...mber last year and ...clips to know what to do ...a childhood dream of ...

...told the ...

understand what I'd found, until I spoke to people who knew...
...e returned to the shop in Berkhamsted where he had purchased the metal detec- and said to the owners he had...
might want to see.
Wesley said...
...were not in circulation... store of wea...

INSIDE THIS WEEK:

Shear joy at Willows Farm

Some of th...

- Iron Age coins may have been buried as an offering during times of disaster

By David Keys
ARCHAEOLOGY CORRESPONDENT

THE LARGEST hoard of prehistoric gold coins in Britain in modern times has been discovered by a metal detectorist in East Anglia. The 824 gold staters, worth the modern equivalent of up to £1m when they were in circulation, were in a field near Wickham Market, Suffolk. Almost all the coins were minted by royal predecessors of Boudicca, the warrior queen of the Iceni tribe who revolted against Rome in AD 60.

The solid gold staters – each weighing just over five grams – were made between 40BC and his...

is likely...
part of...
individu...
was buried...
of a poli...
natural...

Althou...
ian gold c...
have a tra...
ings of ot...
their maj...
tisham in...
buried at...
jewellery,...
Significan...
within a re...

The new...
important...
probable po...
gious impo...
southern fr...
near its bor...

Chapter 1

Introduction

Treasure hunters to coin it in after find

A farmer's son used milking buckets to collect Britain's biggest find of Roman silver denarii coins – which he began uncovering after using a metal detector for the first time, an inquest heard yesterday.

The huge hoard of 9,310 coins dating from 31BC was found 10in below the surface of a field of barley stubble on 400-acre Northbrook Farm at Shapwick, near Glastonbury, Somerset, in August last year.

Details of the nationally-important find were revealed for the first time yesterday when Somerset coroner Mr Michael Rose ... inquest in Taunton

www.stalbansreview.co.uk   0844 4993225

Above, a coin afte ... and left, the clea ...

Detector user foun ... old on first attem ...

Gardener digs up £1¾m

A RETIRED gardener is to get hundreds of thousands of pounds for Roman treasure he found while hunting for a farmer's lost tools with a metal detector.

Eric Lawes, 69, is to split the British Museum's £1,750,000

reward with farmer Peter Watling who had asked his help to find the tools on his land at Hoxne, Suffolk.

The Hoxne Hoard – 200 gold and silver objects and 15,000 coins – is thought to have been buried about 1,600 years ago. It has

taken the museum two years to raise the cash in gifts and loans for what is the finest such collection to be found in the UK.

Mr Lawes is considering buying a new home in Dedham to make his wife, who suffers from arthritis, more comfortable.

... orsey ... ondon.newsquest.co.uk

who found 159 Roman coins ... ridge had been using a metal ... ... the discovery.
... ey Carrington found the ... believed to be one of the ... t of its kind found in the UK, ... ober last year.
... otal, 159 coins were found in ...

literally only about seven inches down.

"It was gold coloured with a Roman figure on it.

"I knew what it was but I didn't know the significance of finding even one of them.

"I just kept going and within 15 seconds it beeped again"

He carried on looking in the same area and managed to find another 54 coins within about three metres of where he found the first.

Two days later he took the coins to the shop where he bought the metal detector to show staff his findings.

Mr Carrington added: "It's not my game so I didn't understand what I had found until I spoke ... who knew.

"I ...

shire and Bedfords ...
He said: "It is ...
dream of as a chil ... treasure.
"It is certainly th ... lar find I have seen ...
"In the ten years ... this job I have onl ... Roman coins.
"You wouldn't ... Carrington] good ... this.
"There are a lo ... have been doing it ... have never found ... stop.
"He s ...

SATURDAY 17 JANUARY 2009 THE INDEPENDENT

a's gold ... earthed

... oard represented ... lated wealth of an ... unity and that it ... e offering at a time ... drought or other

... first major Icen- ... und, the tribe did ... king votive offer- ... jects. At one of ... centres, Snet- ... orfolk, the tribe ... and arm torcs. ... ere also buried ... losure.

... is particularly ... highlights the ... omic and reli- ... an area on the ... ian territory, ... neighbour

Trinovantian tri ... Wickham Market ... Suffolk where the ... seems to have been ... tance in Iron Age tim ... few miles of the fin ... other important Iron ... larger was a vast, triple ... si-urban centre where ... tile manufacturers work ... dence of mysterious ritua ... human skulls.

The second site was a pro ... ket where dozens of Iron Age ... silver-plated, mainly Iceni ... have been found over the yea ...

"The [new] hoard is ab ... unique," said Ian Leins, the ... Museum's curator of Iron Age co ... is the largest hoard of British Iro ... gold coins to be studied i ...

Treasure-hunters dig up a fortune

Two men who found a hoard of Roman silver coins in a cornfield said yesterday they soaked them in rust remover and hid them under a mattress for safety before handing ... to the police.
... a metal

Roman silver hoard worth ... mint

The men told the inquest th ... kept silent about their find ... several days, returning each da ... unearth more of the hoard. ... when they were satisfied the ... found most of the coins di ... report their discovery to the ...

The one person in who ... confided was the farmer, Mr ... Webb, who had give ... permission to search the fie ... a Roman villa once stoo ...

PLOUGHED

"They came round in ... afternoon after findin ... dozen or so coins," Mr ... "I was half asleep and ... pleased.

"But I soon woke u ... what they had found ... Later that wee ... ploughed the field f ... their search. As t

Unearthing the past

Every so often a remarkable discovery hits the headlines: often a story of treasure hunters striking lucky after years of searching the land, or perhaps a chance find made by a farmer after ploughing. Our imaginations are captured by newspaper stories of hidden piles of gold and silver and the testimonies of their finders. We want to know what will happen to these treasures next and what light they shed upon the past. There is a particular interest in large hoards: the sheer number of pieces may suggest great wealth and hints at mysterious circumstances surrounding their burial.

Stories of the discovery of hoards and people's fascination with them are recorded from the time when an interest in the past and its remains began to be documented. However, we know that people have been finding hoards since the practice of burying them began. They were unearthed while working the soil or clearing land and were exposed by fallen trees or eroded river banks. Places that held significance for people did so over long periods and were the scene for repeated encounters with the past, even if this past was not clearly understood. Bronze Age objects appear in Iron Age hoards, and the Romans in particular seem to have found ancient objects intriguing: fossils and prehistoric weapons were buried alongside their own artefacts as offerings on temple sites. In Britain's historic town centres today, the past lies just below our feet and is revealed

Previous pages
Discoveries of treasure make dramatic news stories, but behind these headlines lie more complex histories.

A group of Roman copper-alloy coins found buried together as a hoard. Controlled archaeological excavation of hoards is necessary for them to be properly recorded and understood.

A late Neolithic group of flint tools, an antler mace head and two boar-tusk blades found buried in a pit in a burial cairn at Ayton East Field, North Yorkshire. Length of macehead 111.5 mm.

when buildings are knocked down or rebuilt. In these urban areas, hoards are usually found by archaeologists excavating sites before they are redeveloped, whereas many recent discoveries in rural areas have been made by amateur metal-detector users.

What is a hoard?

So what do we mean when we talk about a hoard? In its broadest sense, a hoard can be defined as a group of items kept together, perhaps gathered all at once or gradually amassed over time. The hoards that survive from the past are those that were ultimately lost or deliberately discarded. It is likely that many more hoards were split up, spent or melted down, leaving no trace to be discovered. Perhaps a typical image of a hoard would be a pot full of

Drawn & Etched by George Cruikshank

Roman Urn, with Coins; found
in Charnwood Forest.

'Roman Urn with Coins; found in Charnwood Forest', drawn and etched by George Cruikshank (1792–1878). Frontispiece to *The Journal of the British Archaeological Association* VII 1852, containing an account of the discovery of the hoard in Leicestershire in 1840.

gold or silver coins, but it need not be a collection of metal objects. The criteria for recognizing a hoard have been closely linked to the legal definitions of Treasure Trove and later the Treasure Act (see Appendix). These definitions and the popularity of metal detecting in the UK mean that most hoards found and reported as such do indeed contain metal items.

Studying hoards

What is it that gives hoards their special character? Are they more than the sum of their parts? With each new find comes a story, or a number of possible stories and unanswered questions. Who did it belong to? Why was it buried or lost and not recovered? Finders of hoards tell of their excitement and curiosity on making their discoveries: they are both a mystery and a window onto past lives. Although we will never usually know the reasons behind their burial, hoards are full of clues that allow us to speculate. These clues are in their contents but also in their containers and the place and manner of their concealment.

The contents of hoards have much to tell us when carefully studied. The act of hiding a group of objects in a pot in the ground or in a bag behind a wall often keeps them in good condition compared to single objects that are rolled around in the soil as fields are ploughed, or worn through handling and use until they break.

A conservator removing surface dirt to reveal painted decoration on a pot containing a hoard of Roman coins from the Cotswolds area.

They may be rare survivals: things that would normally be melted down for recycling or coins that would have been recalled by the authorities had they not been hidden away. There is fascination and pleasure, too, in a large quantity of similar things. A vast number of silver coins may tell a story of considerable wealth or devastating loss. For those studying them, there is a chance that a rarity may lurk within: new coin types are more likely to be discovered in a sizeable hoard. Having a great amount of one item can sometimes help us to understand it better and to compare it to other examples.

Hoards can be important sources of dating evidence. If a hoard was buried on one occasion rather than being gradually added to, then it forms a 'time capsule' of that moment. We know that this happened at some time after the date of the latest object in the hoard (say, a coin) and this may allow us to estimate the age of other items in the hoard. These sorts of arguments form the foundations for dating sequences of objects and coinage and are often revised when new discoveries are made. A hoard can also show connections between past societies who were in contact or traded with each other, or who perhaps were raided in times of conflict.

Archaeologists have come to realize that the key to understanding a hoard is usually held not in the group of objects itself but in its context, that is, in the information held in the soil immediately around it and the evidence for human activity in the wider landscape. Where the find-spots of hoards have been investigated further, their stories are enriched with detail. Although metal items may be thrown up to the surface by the plough, archaeological remains are often waiting to be discovered below ground.

Why were hoards buried?

There are many theories as to why hoards were buried in the past and the most sensible answer to this question is that there is no single reason. Hoards are often categorized according to the supposed reasons for their burial and this book examines examples of these different types. It is important to recognize that, by classifying a hoard in this way, only one interpretation of past events is being suggested. This book aims to show how some theories are more popular for certain periods of the past than others, and how they have changed according to trends in archaeological thought.

Some of the smaller hoards we find were certainly accidental losses, or purse hoards. This may be the case for groups of a few

The Frome hoard of late third-century Roman coins during excavation.

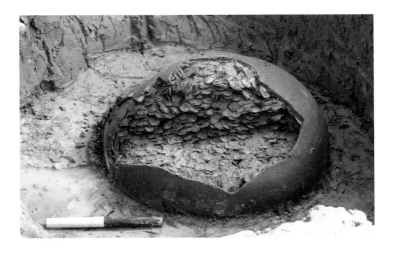

coins found together, sometimes still with the remains of the purse or bag that contained them. Larger hoards are more difficult to interpret however. One popular explanation is that they were emergency hoards hidden in times of conflict, when people who owned precious objects had to flee their homes in a hurry, or felt under threat from raids on their property. This certainly seems to be the case in periods such as the English Civil War, when we have enough historical information to date hoards accurately. The insecurity that war brings leads to a loss of confidence in the usual methods of keeping valuables safe, as in the case of the Hackney hoard in Chapter 5. Of course, hoards were not always buried by their owners: they were sometimes the spoils of war or proceeds of theft and as such needed to be concealed.

Conflict and economic insecurity often go hand-in-hand and are difficult to disentangle. Such a combination of factors may partly explain why so many hoards were buried in late third-century Britain, among them the vast Cunetio and Frome hoards discussed in Chapter 3. Instability in the Roman Empire led to rapid inflation and the official coinage decreased in silver content, to the point where the coins had little intrinsic value. When the coinage was eventually reformed, older coins may not have been acceptable for official payments and this could have been one reason why coins were discarded or hoards were not recovered. This is perhaps familiar to anyone who has saved old coins in a jar and found that they were no longer accepted after changes to the coinage. It is important to remember, then, that hoards may have been buried at a somewhat later date than that of their contents and that the items in them were not necessarily of great value to their owner.

The handle of a silver pan from the second-century Backworth hoard inlaid with a gold inscription recording its dedication as a votive offering to the Matres (mother goddesses) by a Fab[ius] Dubit[atus]. Length of handle c. 110 mm.

Alternatively, their value might have been in the raw material rather than in their face value: a number of hoards are clearly collections of metal put aside for recycling. Such hoards are sometimes described as founders' hoards. This used to be a popular explanation for Bronze Age metalwork hoards, such as the huge Isleham hoard discussed in Chapter 2, but is the subject of much debate. This interpretation of objects destined to be recycled has also been given to later hoards such as the Roman Snettisham jeweller's hoard (Chapter 3). This could equally be seen as jeweller's stock, as in the case of the Cheapside hoard (Chapter 5).

Concealing coins and valuable items would have been more common before ordinary people had access to banks. Savings would need to be kept secure and hidden until required. It is clear that many hoards started off this way and are sometimes referred to as savings hoards. The Beau Street hoard of over 17,500 coins found in Bath in 2007 (Chapter 3) is composed of eight money bags that appear to have been sorted before being stored in a stone-lined space under the floor of a Roman building. The fact that some of the bags contain earlier coins suggests that the hoard was added to gradually and could represent savings made by a wealthy individual or business. Its proximity to an important religious site could indicate a different source of wealth, perhaps offerings taken from the temple or sacred spring. Again, the reason why the hoard was not recovered is uncertain: maybe the owner died or became ill before it could be retrieved. It is important to remember that not all hoards found in the ground had been buried there: many hoards from Roman villas were hidden in walls or roofs that later collapsed and decayed, or were concealed in these ruins after they had fallen out of use.

Other reasons for the burial of hoards may seem less pragmatic to us. A strong theme that runs throughout prehistory is the practice of deliberate deposition. Putting something underground or in water was perhaps a way of releasing it to the gods, just as burying a body allowed it to travel to the afterlife. Items were sometimes deliberately damaged before being deposited, possibly to prevent anyone from taking them, or to 'kill' them so they could be treated like the human dead. Giving objects to the gods might have meant that they could not be removed by anyone else without dire consequences and so remained where they were placed. There are no records to allow us ever to know the exact meaning of prehistoric rituals but by the Roman period some offerings are accompanied by inscriptions dedicating them to the gods. Such votive offerings may have been made on one occasion or built up over a long period of time, just as coins accumulate when they are thrown into wells.

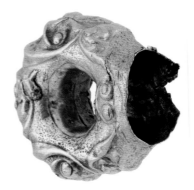

Hollow terminal of a gold torc from Snettisham. This deliberate damage to the object took place prior to its burial in a hoard. Length 44 mm.

We also need to remember that what we might see as unusual rituals were often simply a part of everyday life. In the Iron Age and Roman Britain, for instance, chosen objects were carefully placed in pits and ditches in settlements as well as at shrines. They may mark the beginning or end of use of a building or protect a significant boundary. Not all deliberate burial or destruction of precious objects necessarily had a religious motive. This behaviour may have had an important social aspect. In some societies, a public destruction or donation of valuable items enhances the status of the person giving them away, as in the custom of potlatch in indigenous North American cultures. These ceremonies may be carried out when there is a change of leadership, to create social cohesion in a time of uncertainty or to mark significant events in the community. This sort of public destruction of valuable objects has been suggested for the Staffordshire hoard of Anglo-Saxon warriors' equipment discussed in Chapter 4.

Collections of objects placed in graves tend not to be regarded as hoards, instead being termed grave goods, but this is a grey area because human remains do not always survive in the ground to indicate that a burial was present, as in the case of Sutton Hoo (Chapter 4). Sometimes deposition of objects happens as part of a funeral rite but in a separate place from or on a different occasion to the burial of the body. It is therefore very difficult for an archaeologist to disentangle these connected motives, particularly in prehistory.

About this book

This book shows the variety of objects and stories buried with hoards from prehistory to modern times. Its scope is the British Isles, drawing particularly on the collection of the British Museum, London, which was often the destination of hoards found in the nineteenth and early twentieth centuries. Today the Museum has a role in administering the treasure process put in place by the Treasure Act in England and Wales, which involves many individuals and museums nationally. Hoards may still come to the Museum to be studied or analyzed, but they are now often acquired by or donated to museums nearer the place of their discovery.

Chapter 2

Prehistoric Hoards

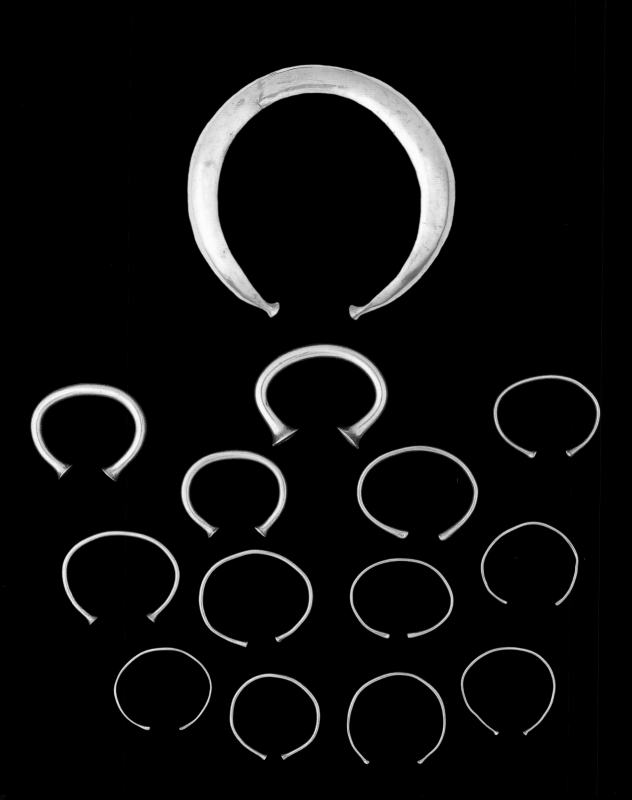

Previous page
Socketed axes from the Salisbury hoard;
Portland type, late Bronze Age to early
Iron Age. Length 95 mm.

Although we now associate hoards with money, people have been storing and depositing precious metal and valuable objects since long before the invention of coins. Hoards of metal objects occurred for the first time just before the Bronze Age in Britain. These earliest finds often contain weapons made of bronze, but gold objects were also hoarded. We will never be certain of the meaning of prehistoric hoards, but it seems likely that the act of placing them in the ground or in water was one of great significance for their communities. The objects contained within these hoards may have been valued for their sought-after materials and the time and skill required to manufacture them, and yet they were intentionally removed from use. The contents and the manner in which these hoards were treated reveals something of this distant past. The examples discussed below illustrate the range of artefacts found in hoards in the British Isles from the middle to late Bronze Age through to the end of the Iron Age, when coinage first appeared.

Gold in the Bronze Age

Gold artefacts were made or used in Britain from around 2500 BC and throughout the Bronze Age. The earliest objects are items of jewellery or personal equipment that are likely to have been highly prized status symbols and are most commonly found buried with their owners in graves (such as the burial of the man known as the 'Amesbury Archer') rather than placed in hoards. Later, from the middle Bronze Age (c. 1500–1100 BC) they started to appear in hoards such as the Towednack hoard from Cornwall, in the form of torcs (or neck-rings) and bracelets, rather than in burials. We cannot be certain that these hoards were not also connected to the burial of the dead, as human remains do not always survive in the ground and were not necessarily buried in the same place as the objects. However, the number of items deposited in the larger hoards implies that they were not just the personal equipment of a single person and may instead be evidence of an event involving a wider community. Simple lengths of thick bar bent into circular forms suggest that the emphasis was on the raw material rather than the display of a highly crafted object.

The largest Bronze Age hoard of gold ever discovered in north-west Europe is probably that from Mooghaun, in County Clare, Ireland. Unfortunately, the full extent of the hoard is unknown, as

Gold collar and neck-rings from
the Mooghaun hoard. Collar
diameter 172 mm.

it was found by workers building the West Clare Railway in 1854, who stuffed as much gold as they could into their pockets; some was sold and some no doubt melted down. They reported finding the gold in a small chamber with a stone on top by a lake. This sort of stone chamber, or cist, might suggest a burial but the manner of discovery means we have no other evidence to indicate that this was the case. The hoard is thought to have originally contained at least 138 bracelets, six collars made of hammered gold sheet and two torcs, and weighed about 5 kilograms. The handful of items that remain are in the National Museum of Ireland in Dublin and in the British Museum. The objects themselves are rather plain in design; they may have been worn both as a demonstration of wealth and as a means of storing them safely. The location of the find not far from a large late Bronze Age hill fort is likely to be significant; it implies a ritual enacted by an organized community with considerable resources at its disposal.

A smaller collection of gold objects was discovered in 2000 in Milton Keynes (Monkston Park), Buckinghamshire. Fortunately, in

The Milton Keynes hoard of two gold torcs and three bracelets found in a pot. Diameter of torcs 144 mm.

contrast to the case above, it was reported by the metal-detectorists who found it and then excavated by archaeologists. This means that we have a clearer understanding of the way in which the hoard was buried and, crucially, the pot in which it was contained. The reconstructed fragments of this shallow ceramic bowl may not be spectacular to look at but they allow us to estimate a date (*c.* 1150–800 BC) for the two gold torcs and three bracelets contained within it, and therefore to similar items such as the contents of the Mooghaun hoard. Two of the bracelets are made from smooth, solid gold with flared ends and the other from a piece that is octagonal in cross section. The torcs appear plain from a distance but are actually decorated with very finely engraved lines. Together, the five objects amount to over 2 kilograms of gold.

Wooden handle and scabbard of a late Iron Age sword from the excavations at Must Farm, preserved due to waterlogged conditions. Handle length c. 120 mm.

Ritual deposition

Deposits of prehistoric metalwork are known to have been made in rivers and bogs as well as on dry land. Excavations at the East Anglian fenland sites of Flag Fen and Must Farm have shown long sequences of finds deposited in places that were not easily accessible, although they were not necessarily remote from human habitation. Bronze Age objects were dropped into fen watercourses from specially constructed wooden platforms or boats. The Must Farm excavations have also uncovered remarkably well-preserved remains from settlements at the fen edge, including huge wooden log boats and many artefacts used in daily life. At Flag Fen and Must Farm the sequence of metalwork deposits extends from the middle Bronze Age to the later Iron Age.

It seems certain that the objects deposited in such watery places were not intended to be recovered. The weapons are frequently bent or broken so as to render them unusable. The damage seems deliberate and to be the result of the application of force, rather than sustained in use. The Broadness hoard dredged from the River Thames contains spearheads that are notched and broken. This is sometimes interpreted as a ritual 'killing' of the object, either removing it from human circulation or perhaps neutralizing its perceived power or spirit. This does not seem too far-fetched if one thinks about the way in which medieval literature describes swords with names and histories, as if they have lives of their own. It is perhaps significant that human remains have also been found in the same places as offerings made in the fens. Were the objects thrown in during the funeral rituals of these individuals (that is, as watery 'grave goods'), or were the humans themselves sacrificed as offerings to a higher power as part of the same ritual?

Small groups of objects buried as hoards could be interpreted as the personal possessions of one individual. A possible candidate is that found at Tarves, in Aberdeenshire, which contained

The Broadness hoard of late Bronze Age spearheads, a knife and a ferrule, found in the river Thames in Kent. Ancient damage is clearly visible. Length of central spearhead 248 mm.

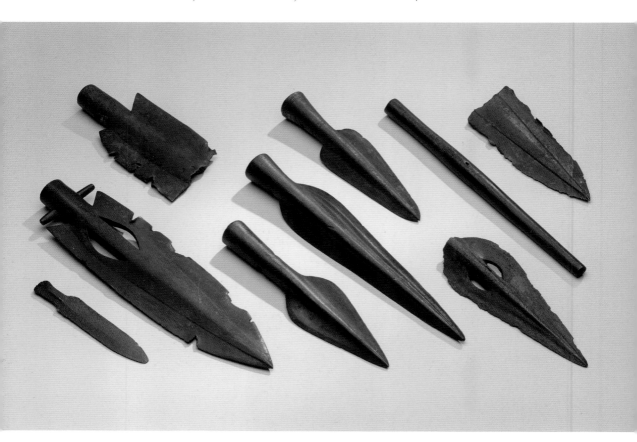

three swords (one with a detached hollow bronze sword pommel), a metal chape from the end of a scabbard and two pins with large round heads (perhaps originally used to fasten a cloak). These pins have a long, slender shaft, which bends at the top in a 'swan's neck' shape behind a flat, circular disc at the head. No human remains were found, and though of course these do not always survive in all burial conditions, these are not the sort of artefacts usually found in graves of this late Bronze Age date in Scotland. Perhaps they were dedicated after the death of a warrior in a special place. The marshy area in which they were found is the type of place that attracted ritual deposits.

Hoards have been found in many other locations besides watery ones. They sometimes occur at fairly inaccessible sites such as mountain tops or in caves. While caves and peat bogs are good hiding places, they could also have had particular significance in past peoples' understanding of the landscape, perhaps as points on the

Part of the late Bronze Age Tarves hoard. From top: pin, sword, copper-alloy pommel and sword, and a chape (the end piece of a scabbard). Length of sword 637 mm.

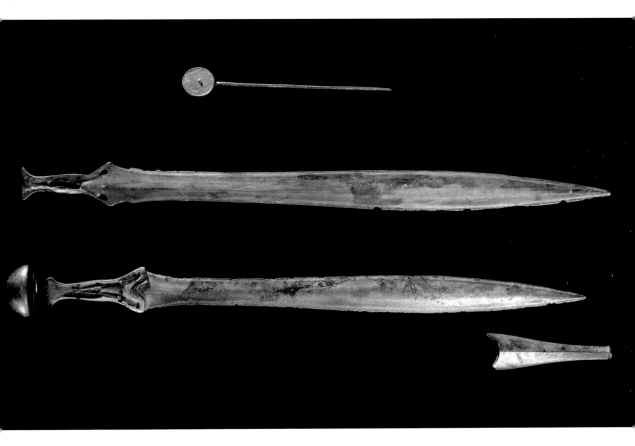

boundary between the human and spiritual worlds. Some continued to attract deposits over a long period, as in the case of the Heathery Burn cave in Stanhope, County Durham. Discoveries made here in the late nineteenth century included Bronze Age weapons as well as objects such as fittings for a cart or chariot, a bucket and gold and jet jewellery. Animal bones and human remains were found too, including three skulls. The archaeological deposits were not excavated using modern techniques and appear to have built up over a long period of time, as Roman objects were also present. It is not clear, therefore, what can be considered to be part of a hoard; some items may relate to burials or settlement activity. However, the presence of at least nineteen late Bronze Age axes is notable, as is the evidence for metalworking: ingots (lumps of raw material) and moulds were present at the site. This certainly suggests that the material from the cave included one or more hoards.

Founders' hoards

The presence of metalworking evidence found alongside weapons may be an indicator of a distinctive type of hoard. Many later Bronze Age hoards were composed of scraps of objects to be recycled as raw material for metalwork and have traditionally been referred to as 'founders' hoards'. These groups tend to include ingots and unfinished items. It is likely that we have here the evidence for smiths at work. This is not to say that these deposits were not seen as having a 'special' character. In some societies the smith is seen as the possessor of supernatural powers. It is significant that these deposits may also contain deliberately broken objects and are sometimes placed in the ground with care and attention to their arrangement. It is for these reasons that founders' hoards are now often seen as a type of ritual deposit.

By far the largest known hoard of Bronze Age artefacts from Britain is that discovered at Isleham in Cambridgeshire, consisting of over 6,500 objects dated to *c.* 1150–1000 BC. The hoard was found together with pieces of an extremely large ceramic pot buried in a pit near the edge of the fenland. When excavated, the pieces weighed about 90 kilograms in total. This hoard has been characterized as a 'founder's hoard' as it contains ingots and metalworking debris, as well as many weapons, tools, vessel fragments and items associated with feasting. Later archaeological work showed that the pot (possibly already broken) had been placed in

A selection of late Bronze Age copper-alloy items from the cave at Heathery Burn: (left to right, top to bottom) sword, spearhead, wheel hub, spearhead, socketed axe, four disc-headed pins, tongs, five rings and a knife. Length of sword 515 mm.

a pit set into a pre-existing ditch, close to what may have been a rectangular building.

The second-largest Bronze Age hoard from Britain was discovered by metal-detectorists in 2007 in Langton Matravers, Dorset. Unusually, the hoard contained only axe-heads, 500 in all. Follow-up excavation of the find-spot by Wessex Archaeology revealed that the axes were buried in four separate pits, possibly located on a settlement site. Some are complete, some halved and others only fragmentary. The axe-heads have an unusual shiny, silvery appearance. When they were analysed, this was found to be due to the high tin content of the bronze from which they were made. This would also have had the effect of making the metal quite brittle and unsuitable for use as an axe in, for example, woodworking. This, combined with the fact that the axes are thin and apparently unfinished, suggests that they were not intended for practical purposes but were instead made specifically as symbolic items to be deposited in the hoard. Although the axe-heads are similar, each one was made from a separate clay mould: a more labour-intensive process than reusing the same mould.

A typical 'founder's hoard' of 145 pieces of late Bronze Age metalwork found in a garden in Eaton, a suburb of Norwich, in 2005. The group includes spearheads, socketed axes, gouges, parts of swords and metalworking waste.

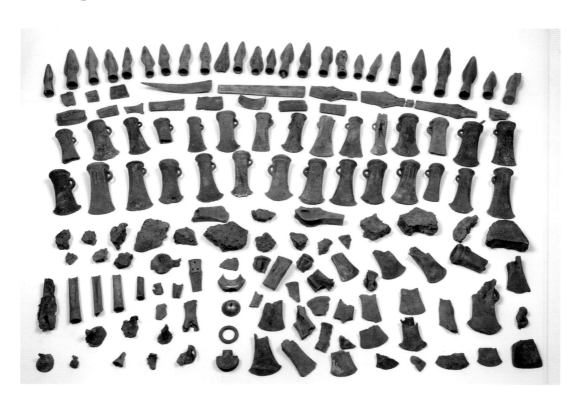

Portland type, late Bronze Age to early Iron Age socketed axes from the Salisbury hoard, similar to those found at Langton Matravers. Length 95 mm.

The hoard dates to the very end of the Bronze Age period, when hoards were deposited in large numbers. It is only possible to speculate on the reasons behind this phenomenon but it does appear to be a time of cultural change and upheaval. Bronze may have been losing some of its prestige value, but iron was still relatively rare. Indeed, it has been suggested that the silvery appearance of the Langton Matravers axes was imitating iron. The period was also marked by a deterioration in the climate, and patterns of settlement and land use shifted as a result. This could have been accompanied by social change or tensions that led to an increase in ritualized behaviour such as the burial of metalwork.

Continental connections

Another large hoard, the third largest from Britain and of a similar late Bronze Age date to the Langton Matravers hoard, was discovered in 2011 in Boughton Malherbe, Kent. It dates from *c.* 950–800 BC and consists of 352 bronze objects and fragments, including weapons, tools, decorative articles and items relating to metalworking (moulds, ingots and waste). The style of artefacts is closer to that found in French hoards, which has led to debate among archaeologists as to whether the objects were made in France and traded to Britain (perhaps as scrap) or whether they were made in Britain as part of the same artistic tradition.

Group of objects from the underwater site at Salcombe, Devon. Copper and tin ingots were found with Bronze Age copper-alloy tools and swords, and gold bracelets and torcs. Length of rapier on the right 372 mm.

The contents of shipwrecks give us direct evidence of the cross-Channel movement of people and objects. A spectacular discovery was made in the sea off Prawle Point near Salcombe in Devon by divers from the South West Maritime Archaeological Group. Middle Bronze Age weapons and other artefacts were found in the area known as Moor Sand in the 1970s and 1980s. In 2004, diving on the site of the seventeenth-century wreck at Salcombe Cannon revealed a further group of Bronze Age artefacts of a similar date (*c.* 1300–1150 BC). Although no traces of a boat have been discovered, it is thought that these items come from one of the earliest known shipwrecks. The finds from Salcombe include weapons (rapier blades and palstaves), part of a cauldron, gold bracelets and many ingots of copper and tin. The sword and axes are of types common in northern France and it has been suggested that the objects may have been in transit from France to Britain, perhaps evidence of early trade networks. These may have extended beyond northern France: one bronze tool of uncertain function may have originated in Sicily.

However, the direction of the trade is by no means certain. The presence of ingots of tin and copper in the hoard may indicate that the load was being carried from Britain to France, as tin in particular is readily available in Britain. Copper, too, is known to have been mined in the Bronze Age at the Great Orme, in North Wales (and has been identified as the raw material for items found in hoards in the Netherlands). The ingots are roughly shaped lumps of metal extracted from the naturally occurring ores. It is tantalizing to think that the ship carried the raw materials (tin and copper)

Middle Bronze Age gold bracelet from the Salcombe find. The band is made up of eight strands of twisted wire. Coiled length 34 mm.

necessary for the production of the prized bronze artefacts of that period. The least visually attractive items in this cargo are therefore the most important ones in terms of what they tell us about the past.

Iron Age heirlooms

Iron Age sanctuaries excavated in France (ancient Gaul) have been found to contain large hoards of weapons, often accompanied by human or animal remains. Towards the end of the Iron Age, model weapons took the place of real ones in ritual deposits made at shrines. These miniature weapons are either of simple design or can look like scaled-down copies of the real thing. Interestingly, some of them appear to be imitating earlier, Bronze Age weapons.

One intriguing aspect of Iron Age hoards is the practice of burying (perhaps re-burying) weapons from the Bronze Age alongside contemporary artefacts. It is only possible to speculate on the meanings that these objects had in Iron Age society: were they prized heirlooms from ancestors, curious discoveries or treated with reverence as examples of skills no longer possessed? Were they perhaps seen as having been made by non-human hands, relics of gods or figures from the distant heroic past? It certainly seems that one of the functions of the sanctuary in the Roman world was as a repository for valuable or simply unusual items. Once dedicated to the gods they could not be removed and were on permanent public display (in some ways similar to a museum).

The Salisbury hoard is one of the largest hoards of prehistoric metal objects ever found in Britain and contains a mixture of Bronze Age metalwork and Iron Age model weapons, buried in the late Iron Age, after about 200 BC. Over 600 objects were placed at the top of a pit cut into the natural chalk in a settlement near Netherhampton, Wiltshire, possibly originally intended as a pit for grain storage. Once such pits went out of use, they were commonly the focus for ritual offerings such as human and animal burials. Certainly, this sort of ritual behaviour was not restricted to 'sacred' sites in the Iron Age but took place alongside the domestic environment.

The large collection of Bronze Age metalwork in this hoard spans a wide date range and included 173 socketed axes dating from 1400 BC until after 800 BC, many unfinished. The earliest items were four flat axes from 2400 BC. The hoard also contained a great variety of tools, such as knives, chisels, gouges, punches, sickles, a hammer and anvil. Unfortunately the hoard was illegally excavated by metal-detectorists and sold to dealers; it had to be pieced together after much detective work by the British Museum and the police. When the British Museum excavated the site of the original discovery it found another hoard alongside it, with parts of a trumpet or similar musical instrument. Traces of a circular ditch were located that might relate to Bronze Age activity on the site before the Iron Age settlement was established: it is possible that later farmers discovered the items in a barrow or in a Bronze Age hoard and re-buried them as part of a larger ritual offering. The fact that they added their own special objects to the collections suggests that this was more than just a re-burial of accidentally unearthed items. The Iron Age items include twenty-four miniature shields dating to the first century BC, some with exquisite decoration, and forty-six tiny model cauldrons.

Impressive though this collection is, its value as archaeological evidence will always be limited due to the circumstances of its discovery. Similar problems of interpretation surround the

Late Iron Age miniature copper-alloy shields from the Salisbury hoard. They have a raised central boss and riveted handle on the back in imitation of life-sized shields. Length of top-left shield 77 mm.

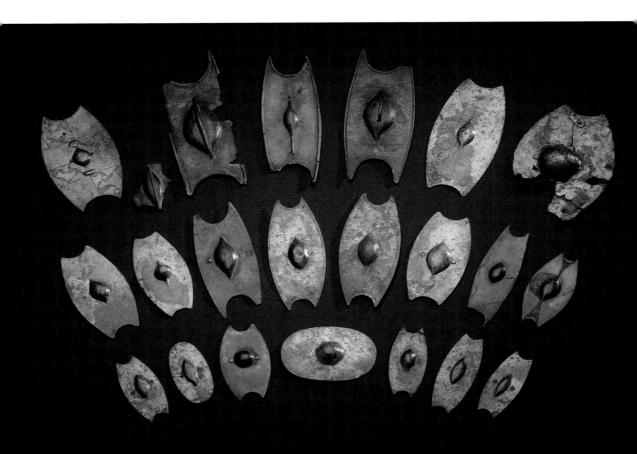

Batheaston hoard, another large collection of Bronze Age and Iron Age artefacts apparently deposited together and now in the British Museum. This is why the hoard from the Vale of Wardour in Wiltshire is so important. Found in 2011 by a metal-detectorist and excavated by archaeologists, it gives us conclusive proof of the hoarding and burial of Bronze Age artefacts in the Iron Age. The 114 weapons, tools and decorative items in this hoard range in date from an early to middle Bronze Age flat axe up to around 600 BC for the Iron Age objects. Unlike the two hoards discussed above, the Vale of Wardour hoard does not include any model weapons and had an earlier date of burial. However, finds made elsewhere on the site suggest that it may have been a focus for ritual offerings well into the Roman period.

A selection of late Bronze Age and Iron Age tools, weapons, brooches and miniature items from the Batheaston hoard. Length of dagger second from top 159 mm.

Horses and feasting

The type of objects that Iron Age people placed in hoards gives us an insight into what was considered culturally important to them. The Polden Hill hoard from Somerset contained many decorative fittings from horse harnesses. Beautifully cast in brass or bronze and sometimes embellished with coloured enamels, these artefacts belong in the tradition of Iron Age art. However, the presence of Roman brooches alongside them dates the hoard to the later first century AD, after the Roman conquest. The elaborate horse fittings demonstrate the significance of the horse in Iron Age culture. Another hoard, from the high-status Iron Age centre at Stanwick, North Yorkshire, included horse harness fittings and a striking bucket mount in the shape of a horse's head. It is likely that these highly crafted objects would have remained in use for many years. A hoard from Westhall in Norfolk contained enamelled first-century AD terret rings (metal fittings used to guide the reins on a horse harness) placed in a bowl said to have been discovered with a Roman coin dating to after AD 138. All these hoards were found in the nineteenth century and unfortunately little is known about the archaeological evidence for their burial. They are usually interpreted as another form of ritual deposit, where valuable items

Copper-alloy horse harness fittings from Polden Hill, Somerset dating to C. AD 50–150 and inlaid with red glass enamel. Length of bridle bit, bottom right, 233 mm.

were set aside as an offering, either for religious purposes or as part of a communal rite.

The cauldrons found in 2004 at Chiseldon, Wiltshire, paint a vivid picture of what communal rituals in the Iron Age might have involved. At least seventeen cauldrons were buried in a large pit along with two cow skulls. The find is currently being studied at the British Museum for the wealth of evidence it holds about the construction and use of the cauldrons. These large metal vessels were capable of holding large quantities of food or drink. They occasionally appear in burials but their presence in a hoard here suggests the aftermath of a feast involving a significant number of people. If this feast had a ritual purpose it might have been considered inappropriate to reuse the vessels. Or the disposal of the expensively constructed cauldrons could have been part of the same lavish, public display of wealth or generosity as the feast itself. Throwing something away or destroying it before it has reached the end of its usefulness sends out the message that you can afford to lose or replace it.

Gold for the gods?

Perhaps the most spectacular find from Iron Age Britain is the hoard (or rather hoards) from Snettisham, in north Norfolk. Uncovered over a period of around sixty years, it consists of a number of separately buried hoards of gold, silver and bronze torcs, coins, ingots and other objects. The torcs are the most striking feature of this treasure. They were first revealed by ploughing in the 1940s, but excavations by the British Museum have shown how they were stacked on top of each other in small pits quite near the surface of the ground. Most of the 200 torcs had been deliberately damaged or twisted together to form composite objects. One of the hoards was slightly different in nature, as it contained fragments of torcs that had been cut into pieces, along with ingots, bracelets and coins, all placed within a metal bowl before burial.

The torcs are of quite different styles; at least one has decoration from a much earlier period and may have been an heirloom at the time of burial. Like many heirlooms, it had been carefully repaired before entering the final phase of its life as part of the hoard. Some of the torcs are made from plain strands of metal twisted together; others are hollow. The most elaborate torc from Snettisham is an extraordinary feat of craftsmanship. It consists of eight lengths of metal rope twisted together, and each length is

Items from the Stanwick hoard c. 50 BC–AD 100. Copper-alloy horse harness fittings and (bottom row) mounts from a wooden vessel in the form of human faces and (centre) a horse's head (length 98.6 mm).

itself made of eight twisted strands. These are capped with hollow decorated ends, one of which concealed a gold coin. The evenness of the strands is remarkable in an object created before the age of machines. Despite the common depictions of Celtic warriors wearing torcs round their necks, they are rarely discovered by archaeologists and a find of this number is unparalleled.

The site at Snettisham seems to have been a focus for offerings made during the late Iron Age and well into the Roman period. It is located on a hill overlooking the coast, in an area rich in archaeological finds. Archaeologists are still making sense of the evidence from the site, which was enclosed by a boundary but lacks any clear evidence for Iron Age buildings. It attracted a large number of Iron Age coins, several of which came from as far afield as the Greek Mediterranean, possibly travelling along trade networks. For some reason, Snettisham acted as a focal point that brought visitors from a wide area and was seen as a suitable place at which to offer precious objects to the gods. The sheer amount of material from the site and the spread-out nature of the deposits make it unlikely that these torcs were simply hidden for safekeeping.

One of the cauldrons found at Chiseldon, Wiltshire in 2004 being excavated in the British Museum's conservation laboratory. Micro-excavation was carried out in order to preserve the fragile vessels and to analyse their contents.

Groups of twisted and fragmentary gold and silver torcs and bracelets found at Snettisham, along with gold coins from Iron Age Gaul. The object above the coins is a hollow tube from a torc (length 67 mm) in which the coins were found.

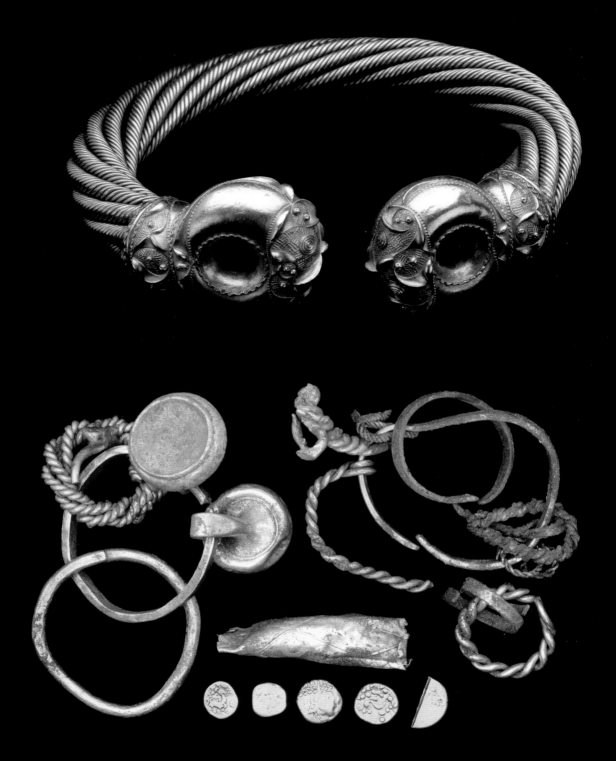

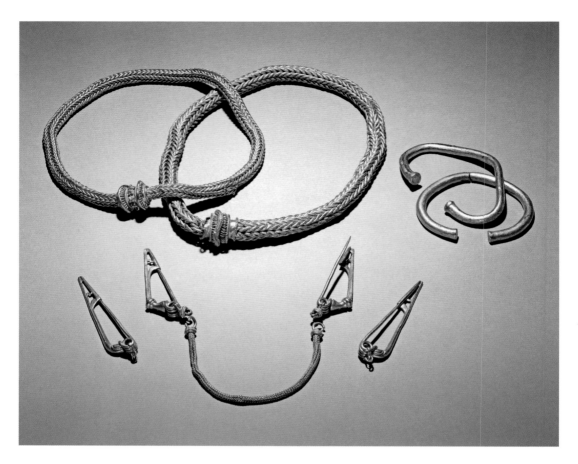

Some rather different torcs discovered in Winchester in 2000 are testament to the cosmopolitan nature of late Iron Age Britain, at least for the wealthy. The two gold torcs were found together, with four gold brooches (each worn as one of a pair, linked with a chain) and two bracelets. The pieces make up a set of matching jewellery for two people but they were not buried with their owners, instead being found on a wooded hilltop. Although they are likely to have been deposited well before the Roman conquest of Britain, they can only have been made by a Roman goldsmith. The techniques used in the construction of this fine, delicate jewellery were unknown in Britain at that time, and had their origin in the Mediterranean area. The purity of the gold is also much higher than that in use during this period in north-western Europe. Who were the owners of these objects? They may have been foreigners but it is more likely that they were wealthy or powerful Britons who

A set of two Iron Age gold torcs, bracelets and brooches linked with a chain found near Winchester. Diameter of largest torc 160 mm.

could afford the ultimate status symbol: imported luxury items or even a personal jeweller. This jewellery was specially made to suit local tastes; torcs like these would not have been worn in ancient Rome. The fact that the items were buried as a hoard suggests that ultimately they served a similar purpose to the torcs from Snettisham.

Currency bars and the advent of coinage

Metal weighed out according to standard units (often in the form of ingots or currency bars) was the first step towards coinage in many ancient societies. As the currency bars became smaller and more portable they were eventually replaced by coins in standard units of weight. In time they came to stand as tokens for these weights: for example, the modern £1 coin, which no longer weighs one pound! In the British Iron Age, iron objects known as currency bars are found in hoards dating from around the middle to late Iron Age. Julius Caesar saw them as part of a monetary system, 'For money they use either bronze, or gold coins, or iron ingots of fixed weights' (*Gallic War* Book V, chapter 12), but this seems to have been a misconception and they are perhaps mis-named (as

Three iron currency bars deposited in the River Nene at Orton Meadows, Peterborough in the Iron Age, along with weapons. The objects were deliberately bent out of shape. Length *c.* 660 mm, width 35 mm.

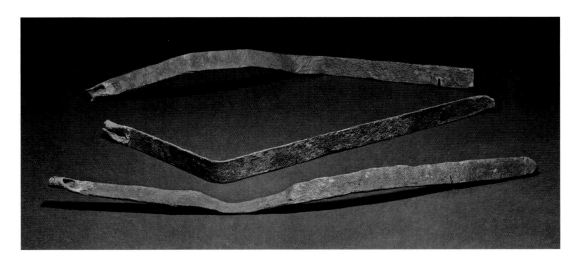

was the implication that they were particular to Britain). Lumps of melted down gold and silver are sometimes hoarded alongside Iron Age coins but the currency bars do not seem to relate to a coinage system.

The bars occurring in hoards are long and flattish, often almost sword-shaped, with distinctively shaped ends. These are variously rolled and pinched, according to regional traditions and (possibly) the composition of the metal. Although there is likely to have been a functional element to their production, as a convenient means of distributing high-quality raw material, their inclusion in hoards suggests that they also had another role. The nine currency bars discovered in the River Nene at Orton Meadows had been deliberately damaged and were placed in a part of the river that had been a focus for deposits of metalwork over centuries. Those from Spetisbury Rings in Dorset were found in a pit in the ditch of a hill fort, along with weapons, buckets, a cauldron and human remains.

Iron Age coin hoards

The earliest coins found in Britain were issued on the Continent, in modern France and Belgium, and may have made their way to Britain through trade or as diplomatic gifts. Greek coins, too, reached these shores in small numbers and occur in some British Iron Age hoards. In fact these Greek coins, or rather copies of Greek coins made in southern Europe, are likely to have influenced the design of British Iron Age coins. When coinage first arrived in Iron Age Britain it was placed in hoards in much the same way as other metal artefacts. The earliest gold coins, in particular, turn up in ritual deposits recognizable from their unusual contents, rather than being found as stray finds on settlement sites. This suggests that they were not used as money as such but treated as prized objects suitable for special offerings, as gifts or other public displays of wealth, as at Snettisham.

One interesting feature of some Iron Age coin hoards is their tendency to be concealed in seemingly innocuous-looking containers. The hoard from Sedgeford, Norfolk was discovered by a volunteer on an archaeological excavation. He was using a metal detector to make sure no metal objects had been left lying on the surface of the excavated area before the project was closed down for the winter, to prevent these being dug up by thieves and causing damage to the site. He noticed a strong detector signal coming from an animal bone, which turned out to be full of Iron Age gold coins, clearly visible when the bone was later X-rayed by a local hospital. Needless to say, work continued at the site until a total of thirty-nine gold Iron Age coins had been found. These were Gallo-Belgic staters, some of the earliest coins imported into Britain from Gaul before local gold coinage was widely produced.

The excavation showed that the cow leg bone containing the hoard had been placed in its own pit, which was then covered by a cow's pelvis. The wider area in which it was found was at least partly enclosed by a large ditch and also included horse burials in pits. Animal burials such as these are frequently a feature of Iron Age rituals associated with both settlements and shrines. The evidence for the latter is often insubstantial in this period, consisting of open ditches and pits for wooden posts, but significant structures can be identified by the intensity of offerings that they attract. This hoard was effectively hidden but its association with animal remains is likely also to have had a symbolic meaning.

Hollow stones were also used as containers or hiding places for hoards. The hoard of fourteen gold coins from Westerham, Kent was found inside a hollow flint nodule in 1927 by a gravel digger on his lunch break. When he poked at the hole with a stick a gold coin fell out; he then poured some tea into the hole and shook it to release the others. The first of several hoards from Chute Forest, Wiltshire was discovered in the same year in similarly chance circumstances, by a thirteen-year-old boy called Victor Smith, who was walking across the fields beating for a shooting party. He threw a stone at a round hollow flint, which broke, scattering gold coins.

The hoard of thirty-nine gold Iron Age coins from Sedgeford, Norfolk was found inside the leg bone of a cow. They were made on the Continent around the time of the Roman conquest of Gaul. Length of bone c. 160 mm.

Remarkably, another flint containing coins turned up in the same place by a metal-detectorist in 1994 and other loose coins have been found in the same area.

The Westerham hoard of fourteen Iron Age gold staters found inside a hollow flint nodule in 1927. Diameter of nodule *c.* 90 mm.

Offerings at the end of the Iron Age

More commonly, the coins do not appear to have been concealed in a container, but are found dispersed in the ground. The fact that Iron Age coin hoards are often found in batches over a period of years may be partly explained by the scattering of coins in the ground by later ploughing, but in some cases it may also be due to them being buried in small groups as separate events rather than in one big hoard. Such a pattern was revealed in detail for the first time when archaeologists excavated the site of Hallaton, in Leicestershire. Although no remains of buildings were revealed on the site, it can nevertheless be interpreted as a sanctuary or similar ritual site due to the unusual hoards unearthed there. They were carefully placed in various locations around what seems to have been the entrance to a large enclosure.

The earliest objects found were gold Iron Age coins buried with the bodies of dogs just outside the entrance. To the right of the entrance was a sequence of Iron Age and Roman coin hoards and, to the left, a whole Roman helmet and other silver objects. The coin hoards were placed in the ground on different occasions; we can envisage a group of people visiting and re-visiting the site and making offerings to the gods there over a long period. Although the latest offerings are well within the Roman period, they respect the space and customs that had existed there before the Romans came. The Roman helmet is a very unusual find in a hoard. It is highly decorated and silver-plated and seems to have been for a cavalry-man. Alongside the complete helmet were cheek pieces belonging to other helmets. Their presence in Leicestershire shortly after the Roman conquest presents a puzzle. Were they perhaps war booty, as is more commonly found in Iron Age shrines on the Continent? Their burial at a site with a tradition of pre-Roman offerings shows that local customs and sensibilities did not die out overnight when the Romans arrived.

Front view of the elaborately decorated, silver-plated Roman military helmet from Hallaton, Leicestershire after reconstruction. There is a female bust at the centre of the brow. Height 407 mm.

Chapter 3
Hoards from Roman Britain

Coinage became widely available in Britain under Roman rule, with large numbers of coins reaching Britain from mints across the Roman Empire. The practice of hoarding coinage continued and coin hoards are relatively common discoveries, particularly hoards of lower value bronze coinage from the third and fourth centuries AD. From 2000 to 2010, over 400 Roman coin hoards were found in Britain. They vary from just a few coins in a purse, to pots so full they would have been impossible to lift. In many ways, the coin hoards of Roman Britain reflect the pattern of Britain's changing supply of money, but they also tell another story about the daily lives of those living under Roman rule. We saw in the previous chapter how the 'hoarding habit' began long before the introduction of coinage and so it is likely that many of the practices behind Iron Age hoards continued into the Roman period, as can be seen at Hallaton (see pp. 46–7), for example. Jewellery, vessels and other items also continued to be hoarded. In fact, some of the

Silver-gilt and silver votive plaques from a hoard found at Barkway, Hertfordshire in the mid-eighteenth century, depicting and dedicated to Mars (left) and Vulcan (right). Height of right-hand plaque 168 mm.

Previous pages
Part of a group of copper-alloy objects deposited in a pot at Felmingham Hall in Norfolk. The items are religious in nature and may have come from a temple site. The figures depict Minerva, Jupiter, Helios and a Lar, with statuettes of two birds and a model wheel below. Height of Jupiter figure 155 mm.

most remarkable hoards from this period are the treasures from pagan shrines found at Barkway (Hertfordshire), Felmingham Hall (Norfolk) and, in 2002, at Ashwell (Hertfordshire). For the first time we have unambiguous evidence for the dedication of metalwork to the gods through written inscriptions on objects.

Early coin hoards in Roman Britain

Before the Roman conquest of Britain in AD 43, contact and trade between northern Europe and the Mediterranean world was well established. Coins from the Roman Republic (issued before 31 BC) travelled throughout Europe into areas beyond Roman control, where they are sometimes found alongside local issues. A silver denomination known as the *denarius* was the main unit of Roman currency from the end of the third century BC right through to the middle of the third century AD. The early coins issued under the Roman Republic did not bear the head of a ruler, but had changing designs relating to Roman history and myth. They were sometimes inscribed with the name of the issuing magistrate, who had a role in the choice of the design. These silver Roman coins had a high degree of purity and continued to circulate in northern Europe long after they had ceased to be issued. They appear in first-century AD hoards in Britain, such as the hoards from Hallaton

Silver Roman Republican *denarius* of 137 BC, depicting the helmeted head of Roma on the obverse (left) and Romulus and Remus suckled by the she-wolf on the reverse (right). Republican *denarii* are found in British coin hoards alongside Iron Age and later Roman coins. Diameter *c.* 20 mm.

discussed in Chapter 2. They were also melted down and recycled as a source of silver for the production of local Iron Age silver coins. Sometimes silver Roman and Iron Age coins were hoarded alongside each other until Iron Age coins went out of use in the middle of the first century AD, suggesting that they were considered equally suitable for this purpose.

The largest recorded hoard of Roman Republican coins from Britain was dug up in south Warwickshire in 2008. Although it contained silver coins issued from as early as 194 BC, the hoard of 1,153 coins was not buried until the middle of the first century AD, because it also included imperial *denarii* up to the reign of the emperor Nero, the latest dated to AD 63–4 . The earlier, Republican coins are worn from a long period of circulation before they found their way into the hoard, and the later coins are much fresher in appearance. This was a great amount of wealth which had ended up a considerable distance from the centres of Roman power. The location in which it was buried is likely to hold a clue as to why it was

The Owermoigne hoard, found in Dorset in 2010, contained four local silver Iron Age staters, three Roman Republican and Imperial *denarii*, and eight bronze Roman Imperial coins dating from the reign of Claudius (AD 41–54).

hoarded. When archaeologists excavated the find-spot they discovered that it was in the foundations of a circular stone building that has been interpreted as a shrine. If so, it shows that the tradition of depositing hoards in sacred places persisted under Roman rule. This is perhaps not surprising when you consider that traditions and beliefs are unlikely to have changed significantly over a period of twenty or so years. However, sizeable quantities of Roman coinage were new to the area, which suggests that the presence of the Roman army was having an impact on local communities.

Hoards from the early years of the Roman conquest of Britain tell us something about the situation in which the Roman army found itself on its arrival in AD 43. A small hoard from Owermoigne, Dorset contained Roman coins from this period, issued by the emperor Claudius. Some of these are copies: poor imitations of the official bronze coinage of Claudius that were perhaps issued by the invading army to fulfil its own needs. There was probably a shortage of 'small change' in Britain for soldiers to use in everyday transactions. This seems to be borne out by our understanding of the local Iron Age coinage: silver and gold coins were issued in a number of regions, but bronze coinage was common only in the area to the north of the Thames at that time and it is likely that exchange and barter systems were used in most communities rather than money. Examples of the silver coinage of Dorset were discovered in the hoard, as well as Roman Republican and imperial silver *denarii*. These three types of coins are likely to have been available in the area before the Romans arrived. The hoard therefore gives a snapshot of the different currencies circulating at the time of the Roman conquest; it may have even been the contents of the purse of a Roman soldier, with a value equivalent to about a week's worth of food. We know from graffiti at Herculaneum, in Italy, that one of the bronze coins would have bought a sausage from a street seller there!

Hoards on Hadrian's Wall

Hoards of gold coins are much less commonly found, particularly in any great number. One remarkable discovery was made at Corbridge, a fort at a crossing over the River Tyne near Hadrian's Wall. Excavations in 1911 revealed a bronze jug, found still upright in the soil. When the jug was lifted by the archaeologist, its corroded bottom gave way and a 'stream of gold coins' fell out. The jug was a flagon with a hinged lid, possibly used for wine. Its mouth was stopped with two bronze coins, which hid the riches below from view: a total of 160 gold coins of the denomination known as an *aureus* (worth 25 *denarii*). This was a large amount of money, about one month's pay for forty Roman soldiers. The latest of the coins is dated to the reign of the emperor Antoninus Pius and was issued in AD 159–60.

This was a significant period in the history of the fort at Corbridge. The AD 160s were the end of a phase of failed Roman expansion further north to the new frontier of the Antonine Wall in Scotland. From this time, the Roman army was consolidating its position on Hadrian's Wall, with a garrison building a new bridge and a more permanent supply base at Corbridge. It could be that the burial of the hoard marked the foundation of this work. Alternatively, it could pre-date it, and represent evidence for a hasty abandonment for a last-ditch (failed) push up on the frontier. High-value coins like these are likely to have been a convenient means of storing wealth to be transported: perhaps sent back home or used

First and second century gold coins (*aurei*) found at Corbridge Roman fort inside a bronze jug. Height of jug 152 mm.

Artist's reconstruction of the Corbridge hoard of Roman military equipment in the wooden chest in which it was discovered. The chest measured 880 × 580 mm.

to pay taxes, or to be changed into lower-value coins that had more practical use. This might partly explain why they were hoarded by their owner.

Another hoard found during archaeological excavations at Corbridge is of a very different sort, but it may also have been hidden during the sudden reversal of fortune suffered by this frontier post. Students excavating in the centre of the Roman fort in 1964 discovered a leather-covered wooden box bound with iron, containing a fascinating collection of armour, weapons, tools and other objects from daily life (such as writing tablets, furniture fittings and a tankard). These had all been neatly packed into the box, possibly for storage during a period of temporary abandonment of the fort. While at first glance they look like the personal possessions of a soldier, other contents like window glass and used iron nails suggest that it was an accumulation of whatever happened to be lying around, perhaps the result of a clean-up to remove all traces of occupation before the fort was left, to avoid resources falling into enemy hands. It was done with care, not haste, however, and some items had been put into bags. The box seems to have been buried deep in a layer of debris left by the destruction of the first fort in the reign of the emperor Hadrian in the early second century AD.

Apart from being an intriguing collection of things that might otherwise not have survived, the hoard is important because it allowed archaeologists to reconstruct the way in which the armour called *lorica segmentata* was put together. While this was already well known from depictions in sculpture, such as on Trajan's column and earlier finds, the excellent condition of the items meant that the finer details of hinges and straps could be studied. The hoard does not contain any complete sets of armour; instead, there are at least six non-matching parts of cuirasses, which may have been discarded or due for repair.

Another, very different hoard of military equipment was found by a boy digging in a garden at Ribchester, a fort in Lancashire, in 1796. Some aspects of this find are similar to those of Corbridge: military items had been placed in a box and buried at around the same time, or slightly earlier, in about AD 120. However, this box contained something that was at the time of discovery quite unique for Britain, and which became known as the Ribchester Helmet. This has a full-face mask in the form of a mythological figure and would have been silvered, creating an imposing and possibly terrifying appearance. It would have been worn by a Roman cavalryman in practice and display games. The other objects in the box are also items that were used by the cavalry, including horse harness decorations, a pair of mesh eye-guards for a horse and a set of pans. This equipment is likely to have belonged to the small cavalry regiment from Asturias, in Spain, known to have been stationed there before being sent to Hadrian's Wall.

Overleaf and below
The copper-alloy Roman cavalry helmet, horse trappings, mortarium, pans and a boar's tusk amulet from the Ribchester hoard. Height of helmet 276 mm.

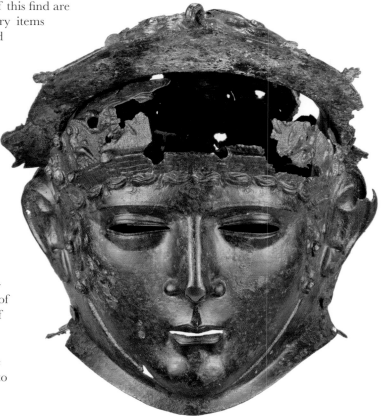

Third-century radiate hoards in Britain

The most common type of coin hoard found in Britain dates from the later third century AD. This was a period of rapid inflation and rising prices in the wider Roman Empire, which was experiencing internal instability and external warfare. The *denarius* had been replaced by the denomination we call the 'radiate' (originally a silver coin with twice the value of a *denarius* but by this time probably worth much less). The nickname comes from the portrayal of the emperor on the obverse ('head') side with a crown of rays in imitation of the sun god Sol. They appear to have been produced in huge numbers and by the AD 270s were roughly, often carelessly, made with almost no silver remaining in the content of the metal. Many of the coins found in Britain were issued by emperors from the breakaway 'Gallic Empire', ruled from Gaul by a succession of little-known emperors including Postumus, Victorinus and Tetricus between AD 260 and 274. The reason that so many coin hoards were buried at this time is still poorly understood but it could be connected to the reforms of coinage under the emperor Aurelian (AD 270–5), who re-unified the Roman Empire, or the more radical reforms under Diocletian from about AD 294, when the radiate was no longer issued.

The process can perhaps be compared to modern changes in currency with which we are more familiar. When a new denomination or currency is issued there is sometimes a phase when the old one is still accepted, but there comes a point when it is not. People may have kept their old coinage and suddenly found it was no longer useful, or hoped that it would one day be accepted on the basis of the weight of the metal alone. Modern periods of hyperinflation have meant that money becomes almost worthless very quickly. Another possible explanation for the spate of third-century coin hoards is that it was a time of great instability, with incursions into the Roman Empire from external groups, as well as endemic piracy and civil war. However, we now know that some of the largest hoards were likely to have been added to gradually rather than being buried in a hurry all at once, so there could be a variety of reasons for their ultimate lack of retrieval. We should not discount ritual motives for some of these deposits; coins continued to be offered to the gods at temple and spring sites such as the Sacred Spring at Bath throughout the Roman period.

The largest known coin hoard found in Britain so far is the

Cunetio hoard, from the Roman town of Cunetio, near Mildenhall in Wiltshire. It consisted of 54,951 coins in two containers: a ceramic jar and a lead box. It was discovered in 1978 by two metal-detector users and the site was subsequently excavated by archaeologists. The hoard was located in a building just outside what were to be later walls of the town. Little is known about the town itself, which dates from the first century AD. It seems to have grown in importance by the later fourth century, when it was finally enclosed by monumental stone walls. This perhaps indicates a significant role in local administration at that time and could be a clue to why such a huge amount of coinage was hoarded there in the third century. Limited archaeological excavation carried out in the area of the hoard suggests that the nearby buildings might have had some commercial or industrial function but these sorts of activities also took place in the temple zones found outside many Roman towns. The coins are mostly base metal radiates from the Gallic Empire and are now in the British Museum, where they form a useful reference collection for the study of other hoards from the late third century AD.

The more recent discovery (2010) of the Frome hoard is still being studied at the British Museum. At 52,503 coins, it is easily the largest hoard of Roman coins found in a single pot. The second was unearthed in 1985 at Normanby, Lincolnshire, and contained 47,912 coins in a pottery storage jar covered by a stone. The sheer size of the Frome hoard has led archaeologists to consider whether or not there could be another explanation for the burial of such sizeable amounts of coinage. It would not have been possible for anyone to retrieve the hoard in one go, as the weight of the coins was more than the pot could have withstood. Perhaps it may not have been intended to be retrieved, instead acting as an offering for religious reasons. In fact, it seems likely that the hoard was made up of a number of separate groups of coins, because the latest coins were clustered in the middle of the pot, where they had been tipped in from another container before the hoard was buried. This might suggest that many people contributed to the hoard as part of a communal collection or offering.

The location of the Frome hoard also raises questions about the motives behind its burial. Geophysical survey of the area has so far not revealed any indication of settlement but there was a spring nearby and the boggy nature of the ground may have made it unsuitable for habitation. There is plenty of evidence for the veneration of springs in the Roman period. The site itself is just below a hilltop and does not appear to be particularly hidden, although of course we do not know what sort of vegetation was there when the hoard was buried. Another intriguing aspect to the site is the discovery of a later Roman silver coin hoard there in the same year. Historic records indicate that there was a third hoard found nearby in the nineteenth century. The position of this is not precisely known but it could have been from the same field or even part of the same silver hoard, as the coins are similar. These revelations hint at a longer-term importance attached to the site. Could it have had some particular significance that made it a suitable place to make offerings to the gods or to bury valuable items with the knowledge that they would not be removed?

The manner in which hoards were deposited is something that is now being given more thought. The spectacular discovery of the Beau Street hoard in Bath in 2007 brought this issue into focus. It was uncovered by archaeologists working on the site of a new hotel in the centre of the city, and was lifted as a heavy block of soil and coins. When the hoard was X-rayed, it was possible to see clear spaces in the mass of coins that looked like gaps between bags

The Frome hoard in its pot during excavation. Traces of plant material wrapped around the pot can just be seen. Diameter of pot c. 450 mm.

of coins. Careful excavation in the conservation laboratory of the British Museum revealed that this was indeed the case. Not only was it possible to isolate separate clumps of coins, but also traces of a powdery brown substance were found forming a layer around the clumps and is thought to have been the remains of skin or leather bags containing the coins. This information would have been lost if the hoard had not been lifted as a block.

The bags that made up the Beau Street hoard contained coins that had been separated out into different denominations. The most recent are from the AD 270s, but the hoard included one bag of *denarii*, of dates ranging from the end of the Roman Republic up to the AD 250s, as well as four bags of the silver radiates circulating up to about AD 260 and three bags of the later, debased radiates. It seems, therefore, as if the money was put aside over a period of twenty to thirty years or transferred from another place, sorted and bagged up. If this happened in the AD 270s, the older coins are unlikely to have been in common use, but they could still have had great value because of their silver content. The hoard is a fascinating glimpse of the wealth hidden within the walls of one of Roman Britain's most famous towns. It is probably no coincidence that Bath was an important religious centre attracting pilgrims from a wide area and even from overseas. The hoard could comprise offerings collected from the temple and sacred spring by the religious authorities, or simply derive from the commercial activity that surrounded this centre.

Silver coins of the denomination known as a radiate from the Beau Street hoard. The hoard was sorted into different denominations and these silver coins separated from slightly later ones with lower silver content.

The final remaining money bag from the Beau Street hoard during excavation of the soil block in the laboratory. The leather bag survives as a powdery brown layer but the coins have retained its shape.

Unusual containers

Most coin hoards from Roman Britain are of a more modest size than the vast treasures of Cunetio and Frome. In some cases, they clearly represent the contents of an individual's purse or a small sum of money lost while being transported or stored. A hoard of fourth-century Roman coins from the Eden Valley in Cumbria (Newby hoard) preserved the shape of the textile or leather purse or bag that it was carried in, even though no trace of this survived due to decay in the soil. The coins had been held tightly in place by the bag long enough to corrode together permanently.

A hoard discovered in 1928 by a young boy digging in the garden in Muswell Hill, London was buried in something that seems quite familiar to us but which was unusual in the Roman period: a money box. It was found in pieces, along with 654 silver *denarii* dated to AD 209–11, a silver spoon and a bronze ring. At first, archaeologists

The Muswell Hill hoard of 654 silver coins was contained inside a purpose-made ceramic money box and buried with a silver spoon. Length of spoon 141 mm.

A money box found in Lincoln in 1851 containing twenty copper-alloy coins from the AD 320s. The vessel was manufactured for this purpose. Height 115 mm.

were baffled when they attempted to put it back together: it appears to be a ceramic vessel that was completely enclosed apart from a slit cut into the shoulder to add coins. The pot does not resemble other vessels of similar date and was perhaps made as a one-off piece for this purpose. Another ceramic money box with a vertical slit was excavated in Lincoln, containing a more modest sum of twenty bronze coins from the early fourth century AD. Such finds seem to be rare, however, and are not likely to have been mass-produced items but instead perhaps made or modified by the person depositing the hoard.

Another way Romans kept their money safe was in bronze arm purses. These are fairly rare finds but seem to have been used by soldiers and a number have been discovered at Hadrian's Wall.

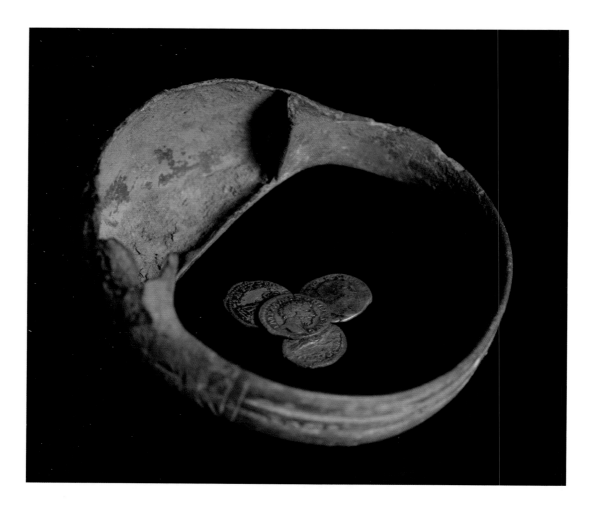

A copper-alloy arm purse found near
Tadcaster and containing four Roman
silver coins of the first and second
centuries AD. The coins would have been
held in place by a hinged lid. Diameter of
purse 109 mm.

They were worn on the arm like a bracelet but had a widened cavity on one side with a hinged lid. A hoard from the Tadcaster area of Yorkshire found by a metal-detectorist contained an arm purse along with four silver *denarii* dating to AD 192 and a fantastically elaborate lamp, cast with decoration in the form of a female head (possibly a mythological figure such as a maenad) and ivy leaves. It is an odd selection of items to lose and seems more likely to have been hidden for safekeeping or placed in a grave; unfortunately we do not know anything else about the manner in which it was buried as no archaeological excavation was carried out.

Sometimes the micro-environment created by a mass of corroding coins will be such that it preserves textile fibres and plant material buried alongside. In these cases we can glimpse small details of the burial of the hoard that might otherwise have been lost. A hoard from Selby in East Yorkshire consisted of two small ceramic beakers packed full of silver coins (99 in one and 102 in the other) and mixed throughout with husks of the cereal spelt, which was commonly used to make bread in Roman Britain. It is not certain if this was added to hide the coins, to stop them rattling, or if it had some symbolic meaning, but it was evenly spread through both pots, which were full to the brim with coins. Another coin hoard in a pot, this time a fourth-century hoard from the Shrewsbury area in Shropshire, preserved fragments of a woven linen textile among the coins. This could be evidence for smaller bags of coins:

The Selby area hoard of 201 silver coins was contained in two small beakers packed in with cereal chaff. The image shows the hoard on display prior to reconstruction and cleaning of the vessels. Height of left-hand pot 67 mm.

we know that coins were sometimes wrapped round with cloth to form rolls tied at each end, perhaps for ease of counting or transport. This was also seen in the Yeovil hoard discovered in 2013. In each of these cases, these details were revealed only through careful excavation by conservators at the British Museum laboratory.

Another way in which organic material may be preserved is through the absence of oxygen in the surrounding soil due to it being waterlogged. This sometimes occurs when a hoard is buried below the water table in an area such as the East Anglian fens or the Somerset Levels. In other conditions, materials like wood will rot away, leaving only the metal parts, such as hinges from a box. A remarkable series of hoards from the peat bogs in the Somerset Levels at Shapwick in Somerset shows the range of material buried as hoards. Here, four hoards were discovered in the 1930s, three of them coin hoards accompanied by ceramic and pewter vessels and the fourth a hoard of vessels only. The first hoard to be found was in a small ceramic beaker that had been placed inside a pewter cup and then covered by a pewter saucer and plate. The preservation in the bog was so good that the mouth of the beaker was still protected by a wad of dried grass; the vessels seemed to be wrapped in dry grass too. With them were two fragments of leather with nail holes, possibly part of a shoe.

James Crane, pictured with the hoard he found whilst cutting peat in Shapwick, Somerset in 1936. This was the first of four late fourth-century hoards discovered in the vicinity and contained 120 silver coins, one ceramic and three pewter vessels and pieces of leather shoes.

Woven textile still adhering to a silver coin from the Yeovil hoard excavated in 2013. The textile survived due to the presence of the metal around it and careful excavation in the laboratory.

Metalworking, recycling and forging

Some hoards were clearly assembled as collections of raw material for reuse. The Snettisham jeweller's hoard is one such example. When a digger operator on a building site in Norfolk came across a complete Roman ceramic pot he was surprised to discover that it contained over 350 individual items despite its small size. When he emptied the pot he found a rich collection of silver and bronze coins, jewellery and red carnelian gemstones. The pot also contained scrap metal, ingots of raw metal and objects that could have been used as tools, suggesting that it had once belonged to a metalworker at the time of its burial in the middle of the second century. Unusually, 74 of the 110 silver coins were *denarii* of the emperor Domitian (AD 81–96), probably selected because they were of consistent metal content and useful as a source of silver. Some of the gemstones were set into finger rings and others were loose, but the similarity of their style indicates that they were carved locally, perhaps in the jeweller's workshop. What is known of the burial site fits in with a picture of a settlement with industrial activity such as ironworking.

The Snettisham jeweller's hoard from the mid- to late second century AD contained 110 coins, silver jewellery, ingots, gemstones and scrap. The items may have been intended to be reworked into jewellery. Height of vessel 175 mm.

Three vessels found on the outskirts of Milton Keynes contained materials for the forging of coins. These were (from left to right): coin blanks ready for striking, pellets and hammered discs of metal, with two iron dies, a lower and upper die. Length of upper die 135 mm.

Hoards show us that coins may have provided the raw material for the production of forgeries. This occurred particularly in the third and fourth centuries when there seems to have been less official control over the coinage circulating in Britain. A remarkable hoard from near Milton Keynes (Roman *Magiovinium*) gives an insight into this sort of activity. Three small ceramic vessels were each filled with materials from three separate stages of the process. In the first pot were bronze pellets made from chopped up cast metal rods, the second contained hammered metal discs used to make coin blanks and the third held finished coin blanks ready for striking with designs. With them were an upper and lower coin die: iron tools for striking the designs onto the coins. However, in this case there did not appear to be any designs engraved onto the dies. For this reason, we do not know the exact date of the hoard but it is likely that it represents the materials necessary to create the so-called 'barbarous' radiates of the late third century or copies of fourth-century coins (known to us as *nummi*). Analysis has demonstrated that earlier bronze coins were likely to have been melted down to provide the raw metal used to make barbarous radiates. This shows that old coins were kept for their value as metal after they had ceased to be useful as money. The hoard was perhaps hidden to avoid this illegal activity being discovered by the authorities.

Changing values at the end of Roman Britain

No discussion of hoards from this period can be complete without mention of the spectacular treasures unearthed in East Anglia that date to the last years of Roman Britain. As a group, they are evidence of the extreme wealth that was present in Britain until the end of Roman rule and possibly beyond. They are also important sources for the study of the art, cultural history and craftsmanship of the fourth century. Many questions are raised by their burial: did they represent items being hidden for safekeeping in turbulent times, or were they belongings of people leaving these shores and intending to return at a later date? Or were they deliberately buried for reasons that are perhaps more difficult for us to understand?

The hoard of late Roman silver plate and spoons from Mildenhall, Suffolk. The Great Dish is shown top left; diameter 605 mm.

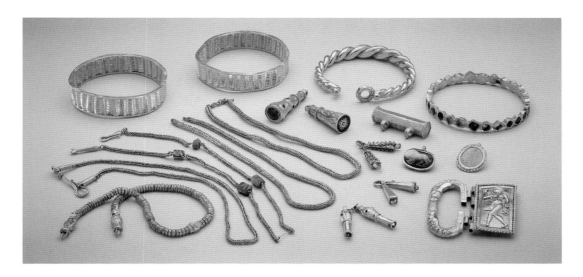

Selected items of gold and gemstone jewellery from the Thetford hoard. Pictured are bracelets, necklaces, pendants and a buckle decorated with a figure of a satyr. The hoard also contained gold finger rings, silver spoons and a shale jewellery box. Diameter of bracelets top left 65 mm. diameter

These hoards can be seen as testament to a time of rapidly changing beliefs and practices. Families would have kept valuable items as heirlooms over many generations, but the public acceptability of religious beliefs altered in the span of a lifetime, according to what was decreed in Rome and adopted in society as a whole. The Mildenhall hoard from Suffolk contains a mixture of Christian and pagan symbolism among its artefacts. The most famous item is the Great Dish, which portrays a riotous celebration of the cult of the pagan deity Bacchus, associated with wine and revelry. This design was appropriate for the centrepiece of a dinner party held by the wealthiest members of society.

The Thetford hoard from Norfolk contained gold jewellery including twenty-two finger rings and several sets of silver spoons, but no coins as far as we know (it was not reported at the time of discovery). The objects have strong pagan associations: a number of the spoons are inscribed to Faunus, a deity associated with the countryside. The decorated gemstones in the rings also have images of pagan gods; here, earlier gemstones are likely to have been reset into later rings. It is an unusual collection of items, possibly a votive deposit, but it is difficult to be certain as its context is poorly understood. It was found next to a wooden building of unknown function, on a hilltop that seems to have been an important site in the late Iron Age and early Roman period. It is thought to have been buried in the AD 390s, at a time when paganism was outlawed in the Roman Empire. This ban may have extended to daily life in Roman Britain; was this therefore an act of dedication or renunciation?

A hoard from Water Newton, Cambridgeshire (the Roman town of Durobrivae) encapsulates the transition between pagan and Christian practices in Britain, with elements common to both religions. It perhaps shows that although beliefs underwent change, the underlying patterns of social behaviour (such as the deposition of metalwork) remained the same. The hoard contains silver and gilt plaques in the same leaf shape as those found in the pagan temple treasures of Ashwell and Barkway but decorated with the Christian Chi-Rho symbol. The phrasing of the votive dedications

The Christogram (Chi-Rho) and alpha and omega symbols on a silver gilt plaque and gold disc from the Water Newton hoard. The form of the objects in this early hoard of Christian liturgical vessels and votive plaques is similar to those from pagan contexts. Length of plaque 131 mm; diameter of disc 49 mm.

on some of the plaques and silver vessels echoes that used for pagan gods elsewhere.

One of the most famous hoards from late Roman Britain was found completely by chance, by Eric Lawes, who was using a metal detector to look for a hammer that a friend had lost while working in a field near Hoxne, Suffolk in 1992. Instead, he found something much more exciting: gold and silver Roman coins, jewellery and utensils. When archaeologists later excavated the find-spot they realized that the whole hoard had been concealed inside an oak chest. The objects were carefully packed, with smaller boxes inside the large one and wrappings of cloth and hay. The box itself had not survived its long period of burial but the metal fittings allowed it to be reconstructed.

The artefacts from the Hoxne hoard speak of a rich and luxurious lifestyle. The jewellery included an elegant body chain that would have been worn over the top of a woman's robes to enhance her figure. There was tableware suited to fine dining: bowls, ladles and wine-strainers and even four elaborately decorative pepper pots (pepper would have been a luxury item, as it was an expensive

Three gilded silver pepper pots from the Hoxne hoard in the form of (from left to right) a hare being attacked by a hound, Hercules wrestling with the giant Antaeus and an ibex. Pepper was a costly imported commodity in the Roman world. Height of central pepper pot 106 mm. See also p. 4.

imported commodity). Unlike at Mildenhall, there were no large items of silver plate. Could these have been buried elsewhere? Combining the two hoards gives an insight into the furnishings of a late Roman dinner table at the highest end of society.

A large number of spoons were found, some inscribed with Latin personal names. There are close similarities with the form and decoration of some of the spoons from Thetford, showing mythical sea creatures. However, there is nothing explicitly pagan in the hoard and some of the spoons are engraved with Christian symbols and inscriptions. Spoons are a common item in other hoards of silver tableware from late Roman Britain and it has been suggested that they had a role in rituals such as baptism or the Eucharist (along with wine, here suggested by the presence of strainers). It is equally likely, though, that we are looking at the treasured possessions of a wealthy family, buried for safe keeping at a time of uncertainty,

Silver spoons from the Hoxne hoard inscribed with the name of their former owner, Aurelius Ursicinus. The set on the right (length 115 mm) have a handle in the form of a swan's head and neck.

A pair of silver straining spoons from the Hoxne hoard with engraved and gilded decoration. This may depict a bearded pagan deity, probably Oceanus, between two dolphins. Length 124 mm.

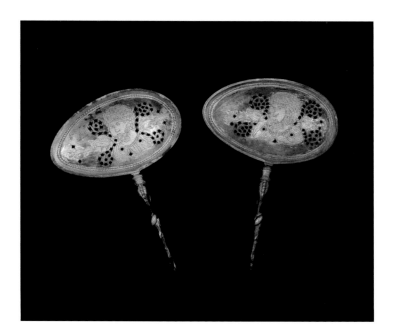

when it was no longer appropriate or possible to publicly display this sort of luxurious lifestyle. The owner was not just rich in terms of Roman Britain; there have been only a few hoards containing more precious metal found in the whole of the Roman Empire.

The hoard can be dated to the early fifth century AD by its gold and silver coins (over 15,000 of them). We know that by AD 410 Britain had ceased to be part of the Roman Empire, but it is likely that there was a more gradual decline in the use of Roman-style objects and coins. Certainly, although no new Roman coins seem to have entered Britain in significant quantities after AD 407–8, the silver coins from Hoxne (known as *siliquae*) appear to have circulated for some time after this, because their edges had been gradually clipped away to remove slivers of silver for other purposes, leaving much smaller coins. This, in itself, is an indicator that Britain was no longer under the control of a powerful state that would have prevented the official coinage being tampered with in this way. The fact that the head of the emperor was left intact suggests some lingering respect. However, Britain was soon to enter a time in which precious metal was valued by its weight rather than the authority it might represent.

Chapter 4

Anglo-Saxon and Viking Hoards

After AD 410 the supply of foreign coins reaching Britain became much more sporadic and there was a gradual shift to the use of a mixture of old coins and gold and silver bullion. Hoards can therefore be quite difficult to date, as objects sometimes circulated for a long period after they were made. In the fifth and sixth centuries no coins were produced in Britain, but this does not mean that it was isolated from Continental Europe. The objects that reached Britain demonstrate the movement of people and cultural contacts that led to the reintroduction of Christianity and the development of strong connections across the North Sea region. Hoards from the seventh century onwards are important sources of evidence for contact, trade and conflict in this area and beyond.

Wealth outside the Roman Empire

Items made and used in Roman Britain appear in fifth-century hoards outside the boundaries of the former Empire. The Coleraine hoard was found in 1854 in Ballinrees, near Coleraine in Northern Ireland. Consisting of a bowl, spoons, ingots, silver coins and chopped up bits of silver objects referred to as hack-silver, the contents of the hoard seem to have had their origins in Roman Britain but are likely to have been assembled locally. The fragmentary artefacts are tableware and military equipment in the highly decorative, Germanic style of the late fourth and early fifth centuries AD. The latest coins are (like those from Hoxne) dated to AD 407–8 but the hoard was probably buried much later than this. As with Hoxne, the edges of the coins have been clipped away, leaving only the head of the emperor visible.

In the gap left by the absence of coinage, other forms of payment were used, and it seems that hack-silver was a means of both storing and transporting wealth. The chopping up of late Roman silver vessels was not a random act of destruction but instead was intended to create portable units of metal. Such items were traded over great distances and long periods of time (the practice continued throughout the early medieval period) and may have eventually been re-formed into objects more to the taste of their owner. The hoard fits into the late Roman practice of gifting large amounts of silver to leaders outside the Empire as a means of forging social connections, buying cooperation, or in return for the supply of troops. It could also have come to Ireland as the result of long-distance trade or raiding. The reasons for its deposition, however,

Previous pages
Part of a large hoard of hack-silver and late fourth to early fifth century Roman coins found in Coleraine, Northern Ireland. Diameter of bowl 189 mm.

are more likely to be connected with its function in local society, whether stored as wealth or deliberately disposed of in a ceremonial context.

Although the Hoxne hoard marks the very end of widespread Roman coin use in Britain, hoards do give us occasional glimpses of the wider world reaching British shores well into the Anglo-Saxon period. The hoard from Patching, West Sussex is a highly unusual collection of Roman coins, some of which may have come over from the Continent, possibly with a Saxon mercenary or trader in the late fifth century. This group of fifty silver and gold coins dated to the AD 460s was accompanied by fifty-four pieces of chopped up silver objects, including a complete scabbard chape, and two gold finger rings. The silver was clearly intended to be used as bullion, as its combined weight was just under a Roman pound. Some of the coins in the hoard were over one hundred years old at the time of their burial and many of the more recent ones are copies of official Roman coins made by the Visigoths in southern France.

Gold and silver Roman and early Byzantine coins, two gold finger rings and hack-silver from the Patching hoard, buried during or after the AD 460s. Diameter of rings c. 25 mm.

Such finds of Roman coins are extremely rare compared to the numbers buried when Britain was still under Roman rule. Coins from the Byzantine Empire were sometimes mounted as jewellery in burials (prized as unusual, precious objects rather than for their monetary value) as opposed to being amassed in hoards, although they are also found singly. A small hoard dated to around AD 475 from Oxborough contained two Visigothic gold coins made into pendants and a pierced Roman silver *denarius* of the emperor Severus Alexander (AD 222–35) that was already over two hundred years old. Although it is known to have come from a grave, this is the sort of collection of coins that might have been worn as jewellery, such as the necklace of beads and coins from the Anglo-Saxon cemetery at Sarre in Kent. Clearly these artefacts had some meaning to those who chose to wear them beyond being lumps of gold, as they are carefully mounted and pierced to hang upright.

Below
The Oxborough hoard from Norfolk. Clockwise from top left: a worn *denarius* of Severus Alexander, a Visigothic *solidus* of Libius Severus with a loop for suspension, a fragment of a silver ring (length 12 mm) and a *tremissis* of Julius Nepos.

Opposite
A necklace found in a seventh century Anglo-saxon grave at Sarre in Kent showing the use of Byzantine and Frankish coins as pendants. The beads are of amethyst and glass, the central pendant a Roman millefiori glass disc. Diameter of disc 25 mm.

The first Anglo-Saxon coinage

In hoards from the late sixth to the early seventh century AD we start to see the Anglo-Saxon kingdoms interacting with their neighbours in trade and diplomatic contacts. A gold pendant found in a small hoard (or grave goods) at St Martin's cemetery in Canterbury in 1844 imitates a coin and is inscribed with the name of Bishop Liudhard, who, tradition has it, accompanied the Merovingian princess Bertha when she came to marry Æthelberht of Kent in the late sixth century. It is likely that these important Continental connections between royalty, the Church and in the active trading system that operated in Britain were the impetus for the local production of coinage.

The Sutton Hoo ship burial included a purse containing thirty-seven Merovingian gold *tremisses* from the early seventh century. As this is a grave deposit, there may have been particular reasons for the selection of the coins in the purse that are obscure to us but it suggests that coins were considered an important part of elite identity at the time. They may even have had monetary use once again, although the purse also contained three blank pieces of the same

Purse lid from the Sutton Hoo ship burial. The gold, garnet and millefiori mounts would have been attached to a leather purse which contained the coins on the facing page. Length 190 mm.

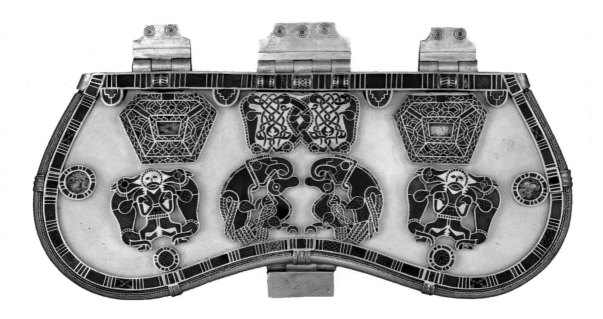

size as the coins and two gold ingots, a sign that the bullion economy persisted. The first coins produced in Britain after a long gap were copies of *solidi* from the Byzantine Empire and Merovingian *tremisses* from northern France and Belgium.

The hoard of gold coins from Crondall, in Hampshire, is the earliest and largest Anglo-Saxon gold coin hoard and shows that coin production was fairly widespread in south-east England by the time of its burial around AD 640. It consists of Merovingian, Frisian and Byzantine gold coins, as well as Anglo-Saxon copies of these issued by rulers such as Eadbald of Kent (the first Anglo-Saxon king named on a coin). As with the Sutton Hoo hoard, this hoard may have been contained in a purse and also included blanks and imitation coins. Just as the first coins made in Iron Age Britain were of gold, the choice of metal here probably reflects its value in long-distance trade and political alliances. The designs feature Roman-style busts and Christian imagery as on Byzantine coins of that period. Some have inscriptions in Latin letters or in a runic alphabet.

Towards the end of the seventh century we start to find a shift from gold to silver coins being made in Anglo-Saxon England. There was an explosion of coin production and presumably coin

The contents of the Sutton Hoo purse: 37 Merovingian gold coins, 3 coin blanks and 2 ingots. The coins were Continental imports.

use, with a wide range of locally varied designs. This must have been the result of increasing demand for coinage of lower value than gold. The Woodham Walter hoard, from Essex, has a mixture of pennies from Anglo-Saxon England, Denmark and the Low Countries. It therefore illustrates the close trading links that existed in the North Sea area at the time of the hoard's burial in about AD 730. Evidence for this busy commercial world has been found at excavated sites such as the trading settlement of Hamwic near modern Southampton. The pennies (often called *sceattas*) were of a similar style and weight and clearly the fact that they were hoarded together suggests that they were used interchangeably. These coins show a convergence of cultures and art styles and innovation in design. The reverse designs are sometimes quite geometric, possibly harking back to Byzantine coin types, but others have a distinctively Anglo-Saxon-style animal ornament on them. Some motifs appear pagan in nature and others feature crosses.

Selected coins from the large hoard of Anglo-Saxon gold coins found in Crondall, Hampshire in 1828 and dating from the AD 640s showing a variety of designs, some derived from Byzantine coinage.

An Anglo-Saxon hoard of silver pennies from Woodham Walter in Essex dating to *c.* AD 730. The varied sources of the coins indicate thriving trade across the North Sea.

Gold from a warrior society

One of the most spectacular discoveries of recent times was made by a metal-detectorist searching an unremarkable ploughed field in Staffordshire in 2008. When local museum staff heard about the find they rushed to investigate the site but unfortunately the gold objects had already been dragged from their original location by the plough and any tell-tale features such as burial mounds had long since been flattened out. It was easy to see from just one glance that this was a hoard of Anglo-Saxon metalwork of the highest quality. However, the hoard yielded its surprises slowly, as the artefacts had to be carefully excavated from lumps of sticky clay. It was not until funds could be raised for the purchase of the hoard by Birmingham Museum and the Potteries Museum in Stoke-on-Trent that the items could be fully cleaned and studied, a process that continues at the time of writing.

The distinctive character of the hoard quickly became clear: this was a hoard of military equipment, with the objects that could be identified consisting overwhelmingly of parts of swords such as hilts and pommels. There were also buckles and sections of at least one helmet of a similar design to the famous example from Sutton Hoo. The decorative style of the fragmentary items varies, with some having fine filigree work in gold or carved interlaced animal decoration and others lavishly embellished with finely cut garnets set into gold cells, a style also used at Sutton Hoo. It is likely that they belonged to different owners and were not made especially for the hoard, but we can only speculate on what they were doing buried in the same field. The hoard does not seem to be a grave deposit; in fact, the sort of artefacts found in graves or settlements (such as vessels, dress accessories or jewellery) are conspicuously absent. Perhaps the weapons were buried there as a monument to a battle lost or won, or in a ceremony connected to a change of leadership. We know from stories such as Beowulf that power was demonstrated and reinforced by the presentation of weapons and other gifts to loyal supporters. Swords like these were not just objects: they held deep meanings and histories that were closely linked with those who owned and made them.

The presence of several Christian crosses in the hoard adds another dimension to the mystery. They belong to a period slightly

Gold and garnet sword fittings from the Staffordshire hoard. The button above comes from a scabbard. The fitting below is from the hilt of a single-edged weapon and has an interlaced animal design.

Gold cross from the Staffordshire hoard, folded before being deposited in the hoard. A gemstone has been lost from the central mount. Length 114.3 mm.

later than the Sutton Hoo burial, around the middle of the seventh century. Two of them are in the form of pendants to be worn on the body but one is a larger cross that is likely to have been displayed or carried in procession. Perhaps the most evocative object in the hoard is a gold-alloy fragment inscribed with a Biblical text that must have had particular resonance in a time of conversion and warfare: 'Rise up O Lord and let Thy enemies be dispersed and those who hate Thee be driven from Thy Face'. Whoever dismantled and folded this object was clearly not moved by these words, if they could read at all.

Viking silver hoards

The largest Viking period hoard found in Britain is the Cuerdale hoard. This was discovered quite by chance in 1840, by workers repairing the banks of the River Ribble by Cuerdale Hall near Preston in Lancashire. The river bank had been eroded by flood waters, causing the hoard to be exposed. The first man to strike

Overleaf
Detail of coins and hack-silver items from the Cuerdale Viking hoard.

silver reported the feeling under his spade as being 'like cockle shells'. The men filled their boots (literally) but later had to empty their pockets and hand in their treasure. The landowner was away at the time and the hoard was sealed up until his return. It was later washed and laid out in a room in Cuerdale Hall.

The hoard has had a complicated life. It was split up after being declared Treasure Trove; most of it went to museums but parts of it were given away to private individuals by the committee tasked with dispersing it and are still being tracked down. A member of the committee even had some items made into a necklace. Its fascination for scholars lies in the diversity of its contents, which come from far and wide: from the Islamic world, to the Baltic in the east and Ireland in the west. As such it is an important source of information about the Viking period economy and trade as well as being studied for what it might reveal about local historical events at the time of its burial, thought to be around AD 905–10.

The hoard seems to have been contained within a lead box, which had corroded and disintegrated, spilling its contents, a vast collection of around 7,500 silver coins and over 1,000 other objects. The large proportion of bullion in the hoard points to an economy that was not yet reliant on coinage. In fact, the silver coins show signs of 'pecking': little cuts and stabs made by a sharp tool such as a knife which were a method of testing the silver content, indicating that the coins were not accepted by face value alone. About one third of the hoard consists of ingots. We can tell that some of these were made from the same mould, suggesting bulk production: impressions left by the mould show cracks developing over the period of its use. Some metalworking waste products were also found with the hoard and appear to have been valued simply as another source of raw metal as they are also pecked. The hack-silver and ingots conform to the same unit of weight, somewhere between 24 and 26 grams. Part of the bullion was formed into wearable shapes, such as arm-rings, to allow people to safely carry and show off their wealth.

The large proportion of Irish silver in the hoard has been connected to the expulsion of Vikings from their trading settlement in Dublin in AD 902. However, the coins were mostly minted under Viking rule in Northumbria and York and the most recent ones come from York, suggesting that the hoard's contents travelled to Cuerdale from York rather than from the west. We do not know who buried the hoard, but it was hidden within Viking territory and therefore could be the direct spoils of raiding parties or wealth built up through trade and exchange over time.

The Vale of York hoard was buried just twenty or so years later

Silver penny of Æthelred II minted in Thetford and found in the Cuerdale hoard. The reverse of the coin clearly shows marks made to test the silver with a sharp implement.

than the Cuerdale hoard, but by this time the political situation had changed greatly: the Viking kingdom of Northumbria was now under the control of an Anglo-Saxon king, Athelstan, who briefly ruled a unified England before Northumbria once again fell under Viking control. It is tempting to see its burial as connected to these turbulent events. Unlike that from Cuerdale, it is a relatively small hoard but no less remarkable in its contents. It was found in 2007 by a metal-detecting father and son and so has benefited from modern techniques of conservation and study. The hoard was completely contained within a remarkable silver-gilt cup and as such formed an undisturbed time capsule dating to around AD 927–9.

The first X-rays of the cup taken at the British Museum showed it to be packed full of metal items. The contents were carefully removed piece by piece in the conservation laboratory before being catalogued. Although small, it revealed a similar variety of artefacts to the Cuerdale hoard, representing the Viking trading world in microcosm. It contained 617 silver coins, 67 pieces of hack-silver

The Viking period hoard from the Vale of York found in 2007. Silver coins, hack-silver and a gold arm ring were found within a silver-gilt vessel. Diameter of gold arm ring 75 mm.

and ingots, and an arm-ring; the latter a rare gold object in a silver hoard. The coins are mostly from Anglo-Saxon and Viking England but some came from the Continent in the form of Frankish deniers. There are also some Middle Eastern coins known as dirhams. These circulated as far north as Britain and Scandinavia through long-distance trade routes by river and sea.

The gold arm-ring is made from a flat strip with the ends twisted together and is decorated with a pattern of punches on its surface. It was probably worn as jewellery and points to a wealthy owner. By contrast some of the plain silver arm-rings in the hoard were probably valued more for their weight in metal rather than as ornaments, although they may have functioned as a means of both storing wealth and showing it off. As with the Cuerdale hoard, the chopped up bits of silver objects such as brooches are evidence

The silver-gilt vessel from the eleventh century hoard from Halton Moor, Lancashire. It is contemporary with the cup from the Vale of York hoard although buried a century later. Height 95 mm.

for the Viking hack-silver economy, where weights of metal were exchanged as fragments or melted into ingots for trade or storage.

However, the most remarkable thing about the Vale of York hoard is its container. The vessel is small enough to be held in two cupped hands and is beautifully decorated with an engraved design picked out in niello (a black silver alloy) and gilding. The design features six different animals set in twisted circular borders around the circumference, with borders above and below of foliage scrolls. The style is that of the Continental Franks, who were raided by the Vikings. They were a Christian society and it is possible that this cup was originally part of the furnishings of a church or monastery, either looted or given as tribute in return for security.

This cup is very like one found in 1815 in a hoard at Halton Moor in Lancashire, which has four roundels depicting alternating lions and unicorns. This hoard was buried nearly one hundred years later, around AD 1025, but the similarity in style is so close that the cup was probably made by the same workshop. It seems that both vessels were heirlooms at the time the hoards were hidden, because their decoration resembles designs seen in Christian manuscripts of the ninth century. As well as the cup, this hoard contained 860 silver coins of the Viking ruler Cnut and a silver neck-ring, showing that silver items continued to circulate alongside coinage in the settled Viking area of England known as the Danelaw. This was perhaps necessary for trading with areas that did not use coinage. Six gold pendants in the hoard show links with Scandinavia. These pierced objects were about the same size as coins but were worn as jewellery.

In an economy where silver was valued by weight, the huge brooches in the Penrith hoard are likely to have been a status symbol. The first brooches from this hoard were unearthed while ploughing in 1785 and 1830 on common land on the hill called Flusco Pike, near Newbiggin in Penrith. In 1989 and 2005, more brooches and pieces of brooches were found by metal-detectorists searching this same 'Silver Field', probably part of the original hoard that had not been recovered. The new discoveries took the form of two separate hoards, one of brooches and the other of coins and jewellery. Clearly, the two hoards had been buried in the same place for the same reason, even though their contents were different.

The brooch hoard contained several complete and beautifully crafted thistle brooches, so called on account of the finely spiked surface of the globes at each end of the ring (a technique known as brambling). There is another such globe at the junction of the ring and the pin. One of the penannular brooches with a flat decorated

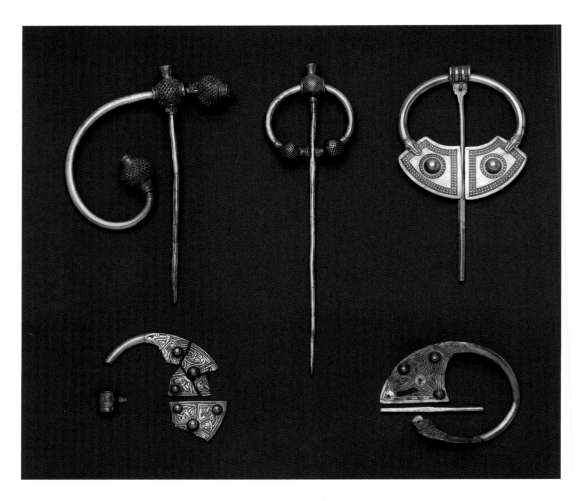

hoop has two inscriptions on the reverse of the hoop, giving part of the Norse runic alphabet known as a 'futhark'. Maybe the act of writing in itself was seen as magical or important. On the largest brooch, the pin is over 50 centimetres long, making it an extremely heavy and unwieldy item to wear. It seems, though, that this was the point; its value was in the amount of silver it contained, so displaying it was a visible statement of wealth and perhaps of social connections between the wearer and the person who had given it to them. In another sense, it was still a portable store of wealth; such objects were chopped up into smaller pieces of bullion to use as money when necessary.

The focus of this chapter has been on precious metal hoards but it is important to remember that other sorts of objects were also

Silver Viking period brooches found near Penrith, Cumbria. The two left-hand brooches, top row, are thistle brooches decorated with brambling. The pennanular brooch top right has a runic inscription on the back. Length of brooch top right 182 mm.

deposited together. The hoard of Anglo-Saxon iron items found in a river at Hurbuck in County Durham is a collection of tools used for woodwork and agriculture dating to the ninth or tenth century AD. A number of such ironwork hoards are known from Anglo-Saxon England. Although they seem like straightforward examples of groups of valuable tools being hidden and not recovered, their deposition may have had different meanings at the time in a similar manner to the founders' hoards of the Bronze Age. The selection of artefacts in this hoard includes weapons (swords), agricultural implements (scythes) and woodworking tools (adzes and axes). This mixing of different categories of objects is shared with other ironwork hoards of the period, some of which were buried in lead tanks. It could have been a deliberate selection or perhaps it was the fact that they were made from iron that merited their particular treatment.

The Hurbuck hoard of Anglo-Saxon iron tools and weapons. Length of top scythe blade 390 mm.

Chapter 5

Medieval and Modern Hoards

Some of the most dramatic stories of loss and discovery come from hoards of the medieval and later periods. Where there is more historical information available to us, it is sometimes possible to speculate on the original owners of a hoard, but the events leading up to its loss and the reasons for its non-recovery may still be shrouded in mystery. That there is a connection between hoards and times of war seems fairly clear, particularly in local conflicts when events on the ground changed rapidly. The English Civil War (1642–51) is the most notable example but there is also a cluster of hoards in Sussex from the time of the Norman Conquest. Even the threat of invasion in 1667 was enough to make Samuel Pepys ask his wife to bury their money at his father's house in the country. His account of their attempts to uncover it four months later is a vivid illustration of how difficult it was to retrieve items after even a short time in the ground; the bags had rotted and not all the gold coins were found. The final story in this chapter gives a similar scenario from much more recent times.

Previous pages
Items of jewellery from the Fishpool hoard. Clockwise from top: signet ring, finger ring with an image of St Catherine, sapphire set pendant, gold heart-shaped brooch, pendant cross (reverse), padlock locket, inscribed gold finger ring, (centre) finger ring with turquoise setting.

Coins of the queen who never was

The Box hoard sheds some light on a somewhat neglected period of English history known as The Anarchy (AD 1135–54). It followed the death of Henry I is marked by instability and conflict over the throne between Stephen, Count of Boulogne, and his cousin, the Empress Matilda (daughter of Henry I, who had declared her heir to the throne). Stephen was crowned in 1135 and had considerable support. The hoard was found near Box, in Wiltshire, in the deserted medieval village of Hazelbury, between 1993 and 1994,

A silver penny of Robert, Earl of Gloucester, minted in Trowbridge, from the Box hoard. The hoard, buried around AD 1142, yielded the first known examples of this coinage.

and contained coins mainly issued under Stephen and Matilda. It is quite likely that the hoard belonged to the owner of the manor, Humphrey de Bohun, who also owned Trowbridge Castle in Wiltshire and was a supporter of Matilda.

The hoard is remarkable because it contained a previously unknown coinage issued by Matilda's half-brother, Robert, Earl of Gloucester, who was the illegitimate son of Henry I but supported her claim. Sixty-two coins of this new series were found in the hoard, issued in the name of Robert and of his son, William, and featuring a lion on the obverse, a device used on the Earl's seal as well. Many of these coins were issued in the faction's power base at Bristol but the hoard also yielded coins from castle mints not known to have been in use at that time, such as Marlborough and Trowbridge. It is therefore of great importance to the history of the West Country at the time it was buried, around AD 1142. By then, Matilda had been driven out of London and Winchester and had fled to the west, which remained her stronghold while the rest of the country supported Stephen.

The poorly written inscriptions on some of the coins issued for Matilda from the hoard show the unofficial and possibly hastily produced nature of her earlier coinage: some are marked PERERIC, thought to be an attempt at IMPERATRIX (Empress, a title given to Matilda on her marriage to her first husband, the German Emperor), and some have had the design obliterated on the obverse side before striking, suggesting that the authority issuing the original coin design was no longer accepted. It seems that Robert was later authorized to issue the new coins on Matilda's behalf, in order to provide financial support for the war. The extent and organization of the coinage and use of the royal lion suggest that this Angevin state in the west was for a time a serious rival to the government in London.

The secrets of Colchester High Street

One of the largest medieval hoards from Britain was found right in the centre of Colchester, when the foundations of a bank on the High Street were being excavated in 1902. The 10,926 coins were hidden in a large lead canister. Remarkably, a second hoard in a lead container from an adjacent medieval building plot remained

undiscovered until 1969 when it was found under a neighbouring High Street building. This second find of 14,065 coins brought the total number of coins to nearly 25,000.

The first hoard seems to have been buried before the introduction of the new, Long Cross type of penny in 1248, as it consisted entirely of the older Short Cross pennies and other coinage. Initially, it was suggested that the hoard had been destined to be exchanged for the new coins, and was perhaps stolen. However, the hoard found in 1969 was made up of newer coins and seems to have been put together in two batches, dated 1256 and 1268–78 respectively. The latest batch was a small 'top-up' of about 2,000 freshly struck coins from the nearest local medieval mint at Bury St Edmunds, which had been placed in the top of the container. This indicates several episodes of hoarding by the same individual(s) rather than a one-off event. The lead canister is likely to have been made especially for this purpose. It was almost full, but had it been so it would have just accommodated a volume of coins up to the value of 100 marks (a commonly used unit of account for larger sums). The amount of money involved equates to tens of

Coins from the second Colchester hoard found in 1969, with the lead canister that contained them. Height of canister 235 mm.

thousands of pounds in modern terms and it is likely that it was held by someone involved in sizeable financial transactions as part of their business dealings, such as a merchant or a banker.

Historical research on the inhabitants of medieval Colchester reveals another, darker aspect to the story, which could explain the non-recovery of the hoard. Houses in the street are known to have been owned by a Jewish man called Aaron, and his sons Ioce and Samuel. At this time the Jewish community was suffering from increasing persecution by the authorities, including demands for levies on personal savings, imprisonment and, ultimately, their expulsion from England by Edward I in 1290. The key dates of the hoards seem to fit in with such episodes. It is likely, therefore, that it would have been necessary to conceal wealth from the authorities and also that events may have overtaken the owner of the hoard before it could be recovered. It is astonishing that a hoard buried so long ago can potentially be traced back to named individuals.

This story in two parts has a postscript. In 2000, building work was carried out on the shop next door to the find-spot of the 1969 hoard, giving archaeologists an opportunity to examine the area. Remarkably, a third lead canister with a lid was excavated only a few metres away from the site of the earlier discovery but this time it was tantalizingly empty: just a single coin was found. Perhaps it had been dropped when the canister was emptied in a hurry. Interestingly, the archaeologists also observed that the pattern on the lead container resembled that of Roman lead water tanks and it is possible that it had been constructed out of one discovered near-by in medieval times (a plausible occurrence in Colchester, which was so densely occupied in the Roman period).

Silver from the River Dove

This substantial find from Colchester pales into insignificance alongside our next hoard, the largest known from Britain of any date. We do not know exactly how many coins were lost at Tutbury but historical records make it possible to suggest that it may have been more than ten times the quantity at Colchester. In 1831, work-men digging gravel out of the bed of the River Dove in Derbyshire began to expose silver coins. They continued to discover more and more, until they were being shovelled out. As the news spread, peo-ple flocked to the site to remove coins, until it was necessary for the authorities to put up notices reminding people that the coins were the property of the Crown and forbidding further searching. There was later an amnesty on coins found and many eventually made their way into the British Museum and other collections. Estimates of the number of coins have been in the tens of thousands and as high as 200,000.

The surviving coins are silver pennies, predominantly of Edward I and II, but also including Scottish, Irish and some Continental coins. From the most recently issued coins the hoard can be dated to the early 1320s and this provides the clue as to what such a large amount of money was doing in the River Dove. The hoard was found a short distance downstream from a bridge across the river and it is likely that the river was forded in this place in the fourteenth century. On one side of the bridge is Tutbury Castle,

Silver pennies from the Tutbury hoard, which dates to the early 1320s.

The Tutbury hoard was found in the River Dove near Tutbury Castle in Staffordshire, seen here in the background. The castle was the base of the Earl of Lancaster, who was probably the owner of the hoard.

situated on a hill overlooking the river. At the time of the loss of the hoard the castle was owned by Thomas of Lancaster, a rich and powerful earl who had taken a stand against the king, his cousin Edward II, in a wider dispute between factions of the nobility in the early fourteenth century known as the Despenser War.

In 1321, the Earl of Lancaster led an army into battle against the king at Burton on Trent. Overpowered and outnumbered, he briefly retreated back to his castle at Tutbury but it was not possible for him to defend it and so it was abandoned. He was finally defeated and captured at the battle of Boroughbridge in North Yorkshire a few days later. During the brief period when the castle was no longer held by the earl, its contents were looted by local people and supporters of the king. An inquisition held at Tutbury in 1323 accused three employees of the earl of having removed from the castle three wooden barrels bound with iron containing £1,500 (about 360,000 pennies). They claimed that the money was being moved from the castle to the nearby priory for safekeeping but it was not recovered. This substantial sum seems a likely candidate for the Tutbury hoard, but how it ended up in the river remains a mystery. It may have been an accidental loss or the river could have been used as a hiding place for it until the trouble was over.

Prized possessions from Fishpool

The Fishpool (Nottinghamshire) hoard of gold coins and jewellery was buried in 1463–4 against a similar background of conflict: the War of the Roses. Like that from Tutbury, the hoard is remarkable for the extreme wealth it represents. The 1,237 gold coins and items of jewellery would have been relatively portable and are likely to have been the personal property of someone in the highest circles of society, perhaps even royalty. The hoard contained four gold rings, a brooch, a miniature padlock, two pendants and two lengths of gold chain (see pp. 98–9). Some of the objects express romantic sentiment and were probably dearly valued by their owner. The padlock is actually a form of locket, to be worn and displayed. It is intricately crafted, with its own key attached by a chain and loops from which up to four pendants could be hung to create an ornate piece of jewellery. The engraved inscription picked out in white enamel on both sides reads 'de tout mon cuer' (with all my heart).

The four rings are of different types. Three have inscriptions, all referring to the heart, which was a popular theme in jewellery inscriptions of the time. There is a plain gold ring decorated with spiralling bands across its surface. While it is inscribed 'uphaf ye ♥ entier', translated as 'lift up your whole heart', this may be a religious motto rather than a romantic one. Another ring has a twisted hoop and a flat rectangular bezel decorated with a figure holding a sword or staff, possibly a saint, and the inscription 'en bon cuer' (in good heart). The third ring is a signet ring, with a heraldic device featuring a hawk's lure on the circular bezel and the words 'de bon coer' (of good heart) inside. This device could identify the owner of the ring (who is likely to have been male) but it has not yet been possible to do so. The final ring is not engraved but it is set with turquoise, which was valued for its powers of protection.

The other pieces of jewellery are a small but fine pendant set with a sapphire surrounded by pearls of white enamel and decorated with a rose on the reverse. There is a pendant cross, with amethysts and a ruby, and probably pearls, now lost. Last but not least, there is a heart-shaped brooch with a romantic inscription on the back – 'je suy vostre sans de partier' (I am yours forever) – and intricate enamel decoration on the front. These French phrases do not necessarily mean that the items were foreign. Although French was no longer widely used among the English aristocracy, these archaic, romantic phrases would have been appropriate on jewellery. There is, however, a possible foreign connection in the coins; unusually, just under a fifth of these were issued in France and

Gold heart-shaped brooch from the Fishpool hoard, decorated with blue and white enamel. It has looped attachments for three pendants at the base, now lost. Length 41 mm.

Gold pendant cross from the Fishpool hoard with a ruby set in the centre and engraved floral motifs on the arms. The reverse is set with amethysts. Height 30 mm.

Scotland and some of them were fairly recent at the time of burial. The English coins are gold and of the denomination known as the noble, and half and quarter fractions of these. They date from the reigns of Edward III (1327–77) to Edward IV (1461–70), and the proportion of newer coins suggests that the hoard was not amassed over an extended period. The sixty-three coins from Edward IV's time include a batch freshly struck all together and as such may have not long come from the mint, perhaps via the royal treasury. This in itself may be another clue to an aristocratic owner with Continental connections caught up in the War of the Roses. The hoard had a face value of £400, which was a vast sum, equivalent to tens of thousands in today's money, but we know that these sort of assets would have been available to the elite of the time. It could even have represented part of the Lancastrian war chest.

Jeweller's stock from Cheapside

In the densely built-up City of London, opportunities to investigate the treasures that lie beneath layers of subsequent occupation are rare and tend to arise only when areas are redeveloped. These are the circumstances of the spectacular find of the Cheapside hoard of jewellery. In 1910, a row of shops was being demolished to allow for reconstruction. Although it was a bustling modern street, the shops had stood on that site since they were rebuilt in 1667 after the Great Fire of London and their cellars reached into seventeenth-century London. The premises were still owned by the Worshipful Company of Goldsmiths, a clue to their earlier history. Numbers 30 to 32 were in a block known in Tudor times as 'Goldsmiths Row' and it was in the cellars of these shops that the workmen's picks revealed glinting gold and jewels in the soil.

What was revealed was a vast collection of numerous pieces of jewellery, decorative objects and the raw materials for making these (such as uncut gems and jewellery mounts). The hoard contained a number of delicately crafted trinkets, of work so fine as to make them one-off pieces probably destined to be sold to the aristocratic elite or even royalty. These included a tiny pendant in the shape of a squirrel carved from orange cornelian, the size of a fingertip; a pin topped with a ship formed from a single pearl with intricate gold rigging; and a remarkable watch encased entirely within a piece of transparent emerald, with an emerald hinged lid. The workmen at first thought they had uncovered a toy shop.

Many of the objects are identical versions of the same piece, particularly lengths of chains, often embellished with fashionable enamel. They could be worn with pendants but were also jewellery in their own right, looped around the body. Such enamel items do not tend to survive well in the ground and they are mostly known from portraits rather than as archaeological discoveries, so this hoard gives us some rare examples. Enamel is seen on a variety of the decorative artefacts, such as delicate handles for feather fans and around settings for more costly gems.

The contents and the location of the hoard make it likely that it belonged to a jeweller working on the site in the seventeenth century, but who? It is surprising, given the abundance of historical records about the street still in existence, that we cannot pinpoint the owner with certainty. This is partly due to the fact that the building plots were further subdivided at that time and as the hoard was not accurately recorded we do not know exactly where in the cellars it was hidden. It could have also been concealed by a thief rather than the owner of the items. However, as the hoard can be dated to sometime after 1640 (by a heraldic badge on a chipped cornelian seal), the owner may have been caught up in the Civil War, or possibly died in the plague of 1665. A name is perhaps unimportant, when there is already such rich historical detail surrounding the place and period of burial.

Jewellery from the Cheapside hoard found in London. From left to right: two gold pendants set with pearls, pendant with bunch of grapes in amethyst, two pendants with amethyst drops, finger ring set with cat's eye, five finger rings set with rubies, emeralds and sapphires, three buttons set with rubies. Length of left-hand pendant 58 mm.

Civil War hoards

In 2011, metal-detectorist Howard Murphy was searching on a farm near Bitterley in Shropshire when he saw a silver coin. Digging down in the soil, he came to a cluster of silver coins in a pottery vessel and realized he had found a hoard. Resisting the temptation to remove it from the ground there and then, he noted the spot and contacted his local Finds Liaison Officer, Peter Reavill, who was able to carefully excavate and lift the fragile container of coins so it could be slowly emptied in the conservation laboratory of the British Museum. It turned out that Mr Murphy had discovered a hoard dating from the English Civil War, buried in a leather purse that had been stuffed inside a type of ceramic mug with four handles, known as a tyg. It was quite small but still held 138 high-value coins of the period: one of gold and the rest silver.

During the Civil War there was a sharp increase in the amount of coin hoards buried and not recovered. These were uncertain

The Civil War hoard from Bitterley in Shropshire being excavated in situ. It dates to AD 1643. Diameter of rim of pot 88 mm.

A receipt for 10 ½ stone of cheese preserved in a hoard of 1582 gold and silver coins from Breckenbrough in North Yorkshire, buried in AD 1644. Width 86 mm.

times and conflict spread rapidly across the country. People are likely to have concealed their valuables when forced to flee or to protect them from armies on the move. The location of these hoards seems to reflect the focus of the fighting in the Midlands and the west of England. Many Civil War hoards appear to have been hidden in haste, close to buildings or inside them (for example in roof spaces of thatched buildings, or within beams), and their owners may have fled or been killed. In the case of Bitterley, the archaeological investigation around the hoard showed that it had been buried in the open, away from buildings.

Coins of this period are accurately dateable due to the fact that the mint stamped a different privy mark on each issue of coins as a way of keeping control of the production process; this usually happened annually. This means that it is fairly easy to estimate when the hoards were hidden. The latest coin in Bitterley is a silver half-crown dated to 1643 on the basis that it was an early product of the recently opened mint at Bristol. The main mint issuing coins at this time was at the Tower of London but the difficulty of transporting heavy consignments of new coins through areas of conflict meant that the supply to some areas dwindled after 1641–3. The areas affected were especially those under royalist control and they started to produce their own coinage, particularly in order to be able to pay troops: a silver half-crown was a day's pay for a cavalryman. Mints sprang up in towns such as York, Shrewsbury, Bristol and Oxford, and issued coins with a royalist propaganda message.

A hoard from Breckenbrough in North Yorkshire gives a remarkable glimpse into life in the royalist troops. Along with the silver coins hidden in a ceramic jug were scraps of documents including a receipt for cheese – 10 and a half stone (approximately 6.7 kilograms) of it in weight – signed by the Deputy Provider General for the royalist forces. This man would have been responsible for ensuring the soldiers received their rations. The hoard can be closely dated by this historical source, but it contains a lack of recent coins, which is again indicative of its royalist context.

Finding alternative sources of silver became important in areas cut off from the main supply (much of the silver being coined at

Four pieces of silver siege money issued during the English Civil War. Minted in (clockwise from top left): Carlisle 1645, Scarborough 1645, Pontefract 1648 and Newark 1646.

the Tower came from South America, via Spanish allies). Native sources such as the mines in south-west Wales were exploited once again. The mint in Aberystwyth indicated that Welsh silver had been used in its coins in the Civil War period by stamping them with the feathers of the Prince of Wales. The need for silver was equally pressing in places under siege. A hoard (now lost) from the important royalist stronghold of Newark on Trent contained examples of unusual silver coins known as siege-pieces. They are irregular in shape – many are likely to have been cut from silver plate called in to help the cause – and are stamped with a design showing the castle in which they were made. Coins were not the only items hidden during the English Civil War: the need for silver meant that anything portable was potentially at risk and people forced to flee would have taken whatever they could carry.

A hoard of seven silver spoons from Netherhampton near Salisbury may well have been buried during this period. They can be dated to 1596–1632 from their marks but they may not have been new at the time of burial. The war is a likely reason for their non-recovery.

The Netherhampton hoard of seven silver spoons, deposited after 1632. They were made in Salisbury at different dates between 1596 and 1632.

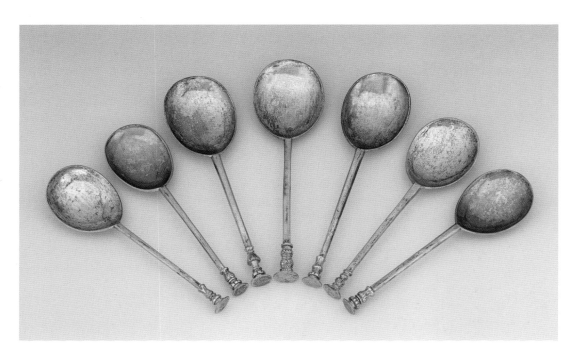

Unclaimed treasure from the 1690s

A curious case of a hoard surviving without being hidden is that of the Chancery Court hoard. The money in the hoard (1,746 silver sixpences, shillings and half-crowns and four gold coins, probably in the region of around six or seven thousand pounds in today's money) was deposited at the Court of Chancery in the late seventeenth century as a suitor's fee in the case of Jones v Lloyd but was never claimed and no details of the case were recorded to enable it to be returned. The money was housed at the Bank of England and slowly forgotten, until it was rediscovered in 1978 and transferred to the British Museum on loan.

The date of the hoard is something of a mystery, given that a single coin, dated to 1696 in the reign of William III, was much later than the next most recent coin, of 1679. The hoard was deposited in four leather bags and a wooden box. The coins are worn and clipped, showing the poor state of the coinage at that time, something that led to the Great Recoinage of 1696, when

The hoard of silver and gold coins from the Court of Chancery, preserved at the Bank of England since the late seventeenth century.

machine-milled money began to replace the old struck coinage of the Tudor and Stuart periods still in circulation.

At this time the Court of Chancery was often criticized for the cost of bringing a case and the tendency for these cases to drag on for years before resolution. More seriously, there were accusations of corruption on the part of court officials who were accused of misappropriating the funds set aside on behalf of suitors. The matter came to a head when the 'bubble' caused by a period of rampant speculation on the overvalued South Sea Company burst and officials were caught out, having invested the Court's funds unwisely and without permission. The scandal led to the impeachment of the Lord Chancellor. After this episode, reforms were made, including the requirement for suitors' fees to be kept under lock and key at the Bank of England. Eventually, in 1726, the unclaimed funds from Chancery were officially transferred to the Bank of England. This was not the only unclaimed case in the Suitors Fund at the Bank but it is likely that a combination of the timing of these events and the reforms of the coinage meant that it was preserved in its original state.

A wartime mystery in Hackney

A recent hoard of gold coins found in a garden in Hackney, east London brings us into the twentieth century. It shows how, even in modern times, periods of great insecurity (in this case the Second World War) can lead to a loss of confidence in the banking system and the hoarding of wealth. This hoard differs from earlier finds in that it was possible to trace the owner and thus explain why it was buried.

The story began with the discovery of a sealed glass jar containing eighty American twenty dollar 'double eagle' gold coins wrapped up in greaseproof paper. It was found while the occupants of the house in Hackney were digging a pond in the garden and they reported the find to the Museum of London, having no knowledge of the owner. Although the coins were less than 300 years old, they would still count as potential treasure under the Treasure Act (see Appendix) if they came under the category of objects buried with the intention of recovery by an owner who could not now be traced. The latest coin was issued in 1913, so the assumption was that the hoard had been buried during the First World War but it was difficult to track down an owner from that time. The find was publicized in the hope that someone with information about the owner would come forward and gradually the mystery unravelled.

A member of the public sent in a newspaper cutting of a similar discovery during building work in 1952, which was claimed by a previous owner of the property, Mr Martin Sulzbacher. Detective work by museum staff began to reveal the extraordinary story of his life. As a German Jew, Mr Sulzbacher had come to England with his family in 1938 to escape increasing persecution. However, when war was declared he was classed as an enemy alien and when the security situation worsened in 1940 he had to leave his home for internment, which sent him first to the Isle of Man and then to Australia (having survived a shipwreck when the ship taking him to Canada was torpedoed).

A wartime hoard of eighty $20 gold coins found in a garden in Hackney in 2007.

His gold coins had been kept in a safety deposit box in a London bank, but while he was away his brother (who remained in the house in Hackney) became afraid that German invaders would raid the banks and so he buried Mr Sulzbacher's coins in the back garden. He told a friend what he had done but not the location of the coins, which he kept secret. Tragically, in 1940 Mr Sulzbacher's parents and siblings were killed when the house in Hackney was bombed in the Blitz. When Mr Sulzbacher and his family returned in 1942 he failed to find the hoard. Eventually the council took over the site of the house and cleared it in 1952, when the first batch of coins was discovered.

Although Mr Sulzbacher had since died it was eventually possible to trace his son, Max, in Jerusalem and the hoard was restored to its rightful owner. His family decided to reward the finders of the hoard and also to donate one coin to Hackney Museum, where it illustrates a very personal experience of the story of Hackney at the time of the Second World War.

Afterword

One of the most exciting aspects of archaeology is that new discoveries continue to be made and often turn up the unexpected. Around fifty Iron Age and Roman coin hoards alone are reported each year. Some of these are additions to existing hoards while others provide the first evidence for Roman activity known in their areas. While this book was being written, over 70,000 silver Iron Age coins were being slowly excavated from a fused mass found in Jersey, gradually revealing secrets such as the presence of gold torcs among the coins.

As these discoveries are made they add to our knowledge of the past and our theories as to why hoards were buried are continually revised. Earlier explanations, such as the use of hoards to map out the spread of hostile invaders, gradually give way to new theories. It is clear, though, that we are very far from having all the answers and I hope that this book raises more questions about the artefacts behind the headlines. The clues to our understanding of the people who buried these hoards and the societies from which they came are hidden in the details of their contents and archaeological context, making it important to uncover as much information about the finds as we can before it is lost to us.

Appendix: The Treasure Act 1996

What is Treasure?

Certain ancient artefacts are classed as Treasure under UK law and must be reported, even if found on archaeological sites. In Scotland and the Isle of Man all objects must be reported. The law in England, Wales and Northern Ireland considers the following items to be Treasure:

1. Any precious metal (over 10 per cent gold or silver) object more than 300 years old, apart from single coins.
2. Two or more precious metal coins over 300 years old that are part of the same find (for example, a hoard).
3. Ten or more base metal coins over 300 years old that are part of the same find.
4. Two or more prehistoric objects of any metal, provided they are from the same find.
5. Single prehistoric objects containing any amount of precious metal.
6. Other artefacts of any material that were found with objects in the above categories (for example, the pot that contained a hoard).
7. Items that would have been considered Treasure Trove under earlier legislation. The main factor here is that the gold or silver objects have been buried with the intention of being recovered by the owner, who can no longer be traced.

What to do if you find Treasure?

In England and Wales the discovery must be reported to the coroner within fourteen days of the find being made (or realizing that it is Treasure). This can be done directly or through your local Finds Liaison Officer (see www.finds.org.uk for details and further information and advice on the Treasure Act). Typically, the objects are then examined by an expert to see if they count as Treasure and local museums are then given the chance to acquire the items if the finder does not want to donate them. If a museum wishes to acquire the items, there will be an inquest by the coroner to decide if they are to be declared Treasure. The objects will be valued by an independent expert from the antiquities trade and a formal value is then recommended by a panel of experts on the Treasure Valuation Committee. The interested museum will pay this sum to take possession of the find, and the finder and the landowner usually share the money as a reward. If no museum wants to acquire the objects they are returned to the finder with the agreement of the landowner.

The Portable Antiquities Scheme

If you find an object that is not classed as Treasure the Portable Antiquities Scheme would still be interested in making a record of it. This is a voluntary scheme allowing finders of archaeological objects to have their discoveries identified and recorded on a national database, www.finds.org.uk. The database now contains over a million objects from all over England and Wales, found by people gardening, metal-detecting and walking the dog. Photographs and descriptions of the objects made by the national network of Finds Liaison Officers form a unique record of the artefacts used in the past and is an important resource for research.

Members of the Treasure Valuation Committee examining the Staffordshire hoard at the British Museum.

Further Reading

Abdy, R., *Romano-British Coin Hoards*, Princes Risborough: Shire Archaeology 2002

Barber, M., *Bronze & the Bronze Age: Metalwork & Society in Britain c. 2500–800 BC*, Stroud: Tempus 2003

Bland, R. and J. Naylor (eds), *Hoarding and the Deposition of Metalwork from the Bronze Age to the 20th Century: a British Perspective*, Oxford: Archaeopress 2015

Besly, E., *Coins and Medals of the English Civil War*, London: Seaby 1990

Bradley, R., *The Passage of Arms. An Archaeological Analysis of Prehistoric Hoards and Votive Deposits*, Oxford: Oxbow Books 1998

Forsyth, H., *The Cheapside Hoard: London's Lost Jewels*, London: Museum of London 2013

Graham-Campbell, J. (ed.), *The Cuerdale Hoard and Related Viking-age Silver and Gold from Britain and Ireland in the British Museum*, London: British Museum Press 2011

Hinton, D.A., *Gold and Gilt, Pots and Pins: Possessions and People in Medieval Britain*, Oxford: Oxford University Press 2005

Hobbs, R., *Treasure: Finding Our Past*, London: British Museum Press 2003

Johns, C.M., *The Hoxne Late Roman Treasure. Gold Jewellery and Silver Plate*, London: British Museum Press 2010

Leahy, K. and R. Bland, *The Staffordshire Hoard*, London: British Museum Press 2014

Moorhead, S., A. Booth and R. Bland, *The Frome Hoard*, London: British Museum Press 2010

Sources

Chapter 2

Barber, M., *Bronze & the Bronze Age: Metalwork & Society in Britain c. 2500–800BC*, Stroud: Tempus 2003

Boughton, D., 'The strange case of the bronzes buried in the Vale of Wardour', *British Archaeology* 129 (2013), pp. 42–8

Brailsford, J.W., 'The Polden Hill hoard, Somerset', *Proceedings of the Prehistoric Society* 41 (1975), pp. 222–34

Britton, D., 'The Isleham hoard, Cambridgeshire', *Antiquity* 34 (1960), pp. 279–82

Britton, D., 'The Heathery Burn cave revisited', *The British Museum Quarterly* 35 (1971), pp. 20–38

Budd, P. and T. Taylor, 'The faerie smith meets the bronze industry: magic versus science in the interpretation of prehistoric metal-making', *World Archaeology* 27.1 (1995), pp. 133–43

Caesar: The Conquest of Gaul, trans. S.A. Handford, London: Penguin 1951

Coles, J.M., 'Scottish late Bronze Age metalwork typology, distributions and chronology', *Proceedings of the Society of Antiquaries of Scotland* 93 (1960), pp. 16–134

Dennis, M. and N. Faulkner, *The Sedgeford Hoard*, Stroud: Tempus 2005

Eogan, G., 'The associated finds of gold bar torcs', *Journal of the Royal Society of Antiquaries of Ireland* 97 (1967), pp. 129–75

Fitts, R.L. et al., 'Melsonby revisited: survey and excavation 1992–5 at the site of discovery of the "Stanwick", North Yorkshire, hoard of 1843', *Durham Archaeological Journal* 14 (1999), pp. 1–52

Greenwell, W., 'Antiquities of the Bronze Age found in the Heathery Burn cave, County Durham', *Archaeologia* 54 (1894), pp 87–114

Gresham, C.A., 'Spettisbury Rings, Dorset', *Archaeological Journal* 96 (1939), pp. 114–31

Harford, C. J., 'Account of antiquities found in Somersetshire', *Archaeologia* 14 (1803), pp. 94–8

Hawkes, C.F.C., 'The Towednack gold hoard', *Man* 32 (1932), pp. 177–86

Hill, J.D. et al., 'The Winchester hoard: a find of unique Iron Age gold jewellery from southern England', *The Antiquaries Journal* 84 (2004), pp. 1–22

Hingley, R., 'Iron Age "currency bars": the archaeological and social context', *Archaeological Journal* 147 (1990), pp. 91–117

Hingley, R., 'Iron Age "currency bars" in Britain: items of exchange in liminal contexts?', in C. Haselgrove and D. Wigg-Wolf (eds), *Iron Age Coinage and Ritual Practice*, Studien zu Fundmunzen der Antike, Mainz am Rhein: Phillipp von Zaberg 2005

http://www.mustfarm.com/wp/wp-content/uploads/MustRead-June2012.pdf

Knight, M., 'Excavating a Bronze Age timber platform at Must Farm, Whittlesey, near Peterborough', *Past* 63 (2009), pp. 1–4

Knight, M., *Must Farm: Must Read*, Cambridge: Cambridge Archaeological Unit 2012

Leins, I., 'East Leicestershire: coinage, ritual and society in the Iron Age East Midlands', *British Numismatic Journal* 77 (2007), pp. 22–48

MacGregor, M., 'The early Iron Age metalwork hoard from Stanwick, N. R. Yorks.', *Proceedings of the Prehistoric Society* 28 (1962), pp. 17–57

Malim, T. et al., 'The environmental and social context of the Isleham hoard', *Antiquaries Journal* 90 (2010), pp. 73–130

Matthews, S. et al., 'A late Bronze Age carp's tongue complex hoard consisting of 352 objects' (2011). Unpublished coroner's report on PAS database: http://finds.org.uk/database/artefacts/record/id/457499

Meadows, I., 'Nene Valley archaeological survey. 2.4: the late Bronze Age and the Iron Age. Northamptonshire Archaeology, University of Exeter', *Nene Valley: Archaeological and Environmental Synthesis*, York: Archaeology Data Service 2009, doi:10.5284/1000170

Muckleroy, K., 'Two Bronze Age cargoes in British waters', *Antiquity* 54 (1980), pp. 100–9

Murgia, A., M. Melkonian and B.W. Roberts, *European Bronze Age Gold in the British Museum*, London: British Museum 2014

Needham, S., 'Milton Keynes, Buckinghamshire'. *Treasure Annual Report 2000*, London: DCMS 2000, pp. 15–16

Needham, S and C. Giardino, 'From Sicily to Salcombe: a Mediterranean Bronze Age object from British coastal waters', *Antiquity* 82 (2008), pp. 60–72

Rainbird Clarke, R., 'The early Iron Age treasure from Snettisham, Norfolk', *Proceedings of the Prehistoric Society* 20 (1954), pp. 27–86

Roberts, B.W. et al., 'Collapsing commodities or lavish offerings? Understanding massive metalwork deposition at Langton Matravers, Dorset, during the Bronze Age–Iron Age transition', *Oxford Journal of Archaeology* (forthcoming)

Roberts, B. and C. Veysey, 'Trading places', *British Museum Magazine* (Autumn 2011), pp. 44–6

Score, V. (ed.), *Hoards, Hounds and Helmets: A Conquest-period Ritual Site at Hallaton, Leicestershire*, Leicester Archaeology Monograph 21, University of Leicester Archaeological Services 2011

Stead, I., 'Iron Age metalwork from Orton Meadows', *Durobrivae* 9 (1984), pp. 6–7

Stead, I.M., 'The Snettisham treasure: excavations in 1990', *Antiquity* 65 (1991), pp. 447–64

Stead, I.M., *The Salisbury Hoard*, Stroud: Tempus 1998

Chapter 3

Abdy, R., 'Worn *sestertii* in Roman Britain and the Longhorsely hoard', *Numismatic Chronicle* 163 (2003), pp. 137–46

Abdy, R. and R. Jackson, 'Tadcaster, 2005 T268', unpublished file report, London: British Museum 2005

Allason-Jones, L. and M.C. Bishop, *Excavations at Roman Corbridge: The Hoard*, London: English Heritage Archaeological Report 7 1988

Besly, E. and R. Bland, *The Cunetio Treasure: Roman Coinage of the Third Century AD*, London: British Museum Press 1983

Craster, H.H.E., 'Second and fourth century hoards found at Corbridge,

1908–1911', *Numismatic Chronicle* 12 (1912), pp. 165–308

Gray, H. St. G., 'A hoard of late Roman coins from Shapwick Heath, Somerset', *Proceedings of the Somerset Archaeology and Natural History Society* 82 (1936), pp. 163–70

Guest, P., *The Late Roman Gold and Silver Coins From the Hoxne Treasure*, London: British Museum Press 2005

Guest, P., 'The hoarding of Roman metal objects in fifth-century Britain', in F.K. Haarer (ed.), *AD 410: The History and Archaeology of Late and Post-Roman Britain*, London: Society for the Promotion of Roman Studies 2014, pp. 117–29

Hobbs, R., *The Mildenhall Treasure*, London: British Museum Press 2012

Ireland, S., *The South Warwickshire Hoard of Roman Denarii*, BAR British Series 585, Oxford 2013

Johns, C.M., *The Snettisham Roman Jeweller's Hoard*, London: British Museum Press 1997

Johns, C.M., *The Hoxne Late Roman Treasure. Gold Jewellery and Silver Plate*, London: British Museum Press 2010

Johns, C.M. and T. Potter, *The Thetford Treasure: Roman Jewellery and Silver*, London: British Museum Press 1983

MacDonald, G., 'The Corbridge gold find of 1911', *Journal of Roman Studies* 2 (1912), pp. 1–20

Moorhead, S., A. Booth and R. Bland, *The Frome Hoard*, London: British Museum Press 2010

Neuberg, C., 'The Cranley Gardens hoard', *Trans. London & Middlesex Arch. Soc.* 23 (1972), pp. 164–70

Painter, K.S., *The Water Newton Early Christian Silver*, London: British Museum Press 1977

Ponting, M.J., 'The Fenny Stratford hoard', *Papers from the Institute of Archaeology* 3 (1992), pp. 52–61

Robertson, A.S., 'A find from Shapwick, Somerset', *Numismatic Chronicle* 16 (1936), pp. 245–51

White, A.J., 'A Roman pottery money-box from Lincoln', *Britannia* 12 (1981), pp. 302–5

Zeepvat, R.J., 'A Roman coin manufacturing hoard from Magiovinium, Fenny Stratford, Bucks', *Britannia* 25 (1994), pp. 1–19

Chapter 4

Abdy, R., 'Patching and Oxborough: the latest coin hoards from Roman Britain or the first early medieval hoards from England?', in R. Abdy et al. (eds), *Coin Hoards From Roman Britain XII*, Wetteren: Moneta 2009 pp. 394–5

Abdy, R. 'The Patching hoard', in F. Hunter and K. Painter (eds), *Late Roman Silver: The Traprain Treasure in Context*, Edinburgh: Society of Antiquaries of Scotland 2013, pp. 107–15

Abdy, R. and G. Williams, 'A catalogue of hoards and single finds from the British Isles c. AD 410–675', in B. Cook and G. Williams (eds), *Coinage and History in the North Sea World c. 500 – 1250. Essays in Honour of Marion Archibald*, Leiden: Brill 2006, pp. 11–74

Blackburn, M., 'Gold in England during the "Age of Silver" (eighth–eleventh centuries)', in J. Graham-Campbell and G. Williams (eds), *Silver Economy in the Viking Age*, pp. 55–98. Walnut Creek, CA: Left Coast Press 2007

Gannon, A., *The Iconography of Early Anglo-Saxon Coinage (6th–8th Centuries)*, Oxford: Oxford University Press 2003

Graham-Campbell, J. (ed.), *Viking Treasure From the Northwest: The Cuerdale Hoard in its Context: Selected Papers From the Vikings of the Irish Sea Conference, Liverpool, 18–20 May 1990*, Liverpool: National Museums & Galleries on Merseyside 1992

Graham-Campbell, J. (ed.), *The Cuerdale Hoard and Related Viking-age Silver and Gold From Britain and Ireland in the British Museum*, London: British Museum Press 2011

Leahy, K., 'A deposit of early medieval iron objects from Scraptoft, Leicestershire', *Medieval Archaeology* 57 (2013), pp. 223–37

Leahy, K. and R. Bland, *The Staffordshire Hoard*, London: British Museum Press 2014

Marzinik, S., 'The Coleraine treasure from Northern Ireland: a consideration of the fittings', in F. Hunter and K. Painter (eds), *Late Roman Silver: The Traprain Treasure in Context*, Edinburgh: Society of Antiquaries of Scotland 2013, pp. 175–91

Mattingly, H. and J.W.E. Pearce, 'The Coleraine hoard', *Antiquity* 11 (1937), pp. 39–45

Warners, E., 'The Halton Moor cup and the Carolingian metalwork in the Cuerdale hoard', in Graham Campbell (ed.), *The Cuerdale Hoard and Related Viking-age Silver and Gold From Britain and Ireland in the British Museum*, London: British Museum Press 2011, pp. 133–9

White, S. et al., 'A mid-fifth century hoard of Roman and pseudo-Roman material from Patching, West Sussex', *Britannia* 30 (1999), pp. 301–15

Williams, G., 'The circulation and function of coinage in conversion-period England, c. 580–675', in B. Cook and G. Williams (eds), *Coinage and History in the North Sea World c. 500 – 1250. Essays in Honour of Marion Archibald*, Leiden: Brill 2006, pp. 145–92

Williams, G., *Early Anglo-Saxon Coins*, Oxford: Shire Archaeology 2008

William, G., 'Hack-silver and precious metal economies, a view from the Viking age', in F. Hunter and K. Painter (eds), *Late Roman Silver: The Traprain Treasure in Context*, Edinburgh: Society of Antiquaries of Scotland 2013, pp. 381–94

Williams, G. and B. Ager, *The Vale of York Hoard*, London: British Museum Press 2010

Chapter 5

Allen, M., 'English coin hoards 1158–1544', *British Numismatic Journal* 72 (2002), pp. 24–84

Allen, M., *Mints and Money in Medieval England*, Cambridge: Cambridge University Press 2012

Anonymous, 'Buried treasure at John Menzies' shop', *The Colchester Archaeologist* 14 (2001), pp. 18–19

Archibald, M.M., 'Fishpool, Bildworth (Notts.), 1966 hoard: interim report', *Numismatic Chronicle* 7 (1967), pp. 133–46

Archibald, M.M., 'The lion coinage of Robert Earl of Gloucester and William Earl of Gloucester', *British Numismatic Journal* 71 (2001), pp. 71–86

Archibald, M.M. and B.J. Cook, *English Medieval Coin Hoards: I*, British Museum Occasional Paper 87, London: British Museum Press 2001

Besly, E., *English Civil War Coin Hoards*, British Museum Occasional Paper 51, London: British Museum Press 1987

Besly, E., *Coins and Medals of the English Civil War*, London: Seaby 1990

Boon, G.C., *Coins of the Anarchy 1135–1154*, Cardiff: National Museum and Galleries of Wales 1988

Brooks, H. et al., 'A medieval lead canister from Colchester High Street: hoard container, or floor safe?', *Medieval Archaeology* 48 (2004), pp. 131–42

Carmichael, H., 'The Chancery hoard', in *The Halbert Carmichael Collection of British Coins*, Dix Noonan Web Auction 12 June 2014, p. 84, http://www.dnw.co.uk/media/auction_catalogues/Coins%2011%20Jun%2014.pdf

Cherry, J., 'The medieval jewellery from the Fishpool, Nottinghamshire, hoard', *Archaeologia* 104 (1973), pp. 307–21

Clarke, D.T. et al., 'The 1969 Colchester hoard', *British Numismatic Journal* 44 (1974), pp. 39–61

Cook, B.J., 'Bitterley, Shropshire (2011 T89) hoard of post-medieval coins and their container' (2011). Unpublished coroner's report on PAS database: http://finds.org.uk/database/artefacts/record/id/430201

Forsyth, H., *The Cheapside Hoard: London's Lost Jewels*, London: Museum of London 2013

Hislop. M. et al., *Tutbury: 'A Castle Firmly Built'. Archaeological and Historical Investigations at Tutbury Castle, Staffordshire*, BAR British Series 546, Oxford 2011

Horowitz, H. and P. Polden, 'Continuity or change in the Court of Chancery in the seventeenth and eighteenth centuries?', *Journal of British Studies* 35.1 (1996), pp. 24–57

Richardson, I., 'Stoke Newington's double eagles: the story of the "Hackney hoard"', *Hackney History* (2013), pp. 38–46

Stephenson, D., 'Colchester: a smaller medieval English Jewry', *Essex Archaeology and History 16 (1985)*, pp. 48–52

Thompson, J.D.A., *Inventory of British Coin Hoards 600–1500*, London: Royal Numismatic Society 1956

Acknowledgements

I would like to thank the following for their help with this book:

Richard Abdy, David Agar, Benjamin Alsop, Roger Bland, Rosemary Bradley, Deborah Buck, Barrie Cook, Nicola Crompton, Stephen Dodd, Lucy Ellis, Marianne Eve, Julia Farley, Henry Flynn, Amanda Gregory, Coralie Hepburn, Richard Hobbs, Thomas Hockenhull, Marilyn Hockey, Maria Howell, Jody Joy, Ivor Kerslake, Janet Larkin, Ian Leins, Michael Lewis, Steve Minnitt, Sam Moorhead, Kate Oliver, John Naylor, Sheila O'Connell, Saul Peckham, Jim Peters, Emma Poulter, Ian Richardson, Ben Roberts, Axelle Russo-Heath, Ashvini Sivakumar, Brett Thorn, Slav Todorov, Dave Webb, Gareth Williams, John Williams, Neil Wilkin, Sam Wyles.

Any errors remain my own. I would also like to thank my husband, Paul Cox, for his support whilst this was written outside of work hours.

Illustration Acknowledgements

All illustrations from the collection of the British Museum [BM] are © The Trustees of the British Museum.
p. 2: © Birmingham Museums Trust
p. 4: BM 1994,0408.33

Chapter 1

pp. 8–9:
The Herts Advertiser, St Albans edition, Wednesday, 6 June 2013. © Courtesy of the Herts Advertiser
The Sun Newspaper, Sunday, 19 November 1992 © News Syndication
The Herald, Thursday, 11 January 2001
The Independent, Saturday, 17 January 2009 © The Independent
The Independent, Friday, 20 November 1992 © The Independent
The Birmingham post, Wednesday, 10 November 1999
The Review, St Albans, Wednesday, 12 June 2013 © St Albans Review
p. 10: Courtesy of the Portable Antiquities Scheme
pp. 11–13: BM 1879,1209.1947-63; 1875,1009.410
p.15: Courtesy of the Portable Antiquities Scheme
pp.16–19: BM 1850,0601.1; 1991,0501.45;

Chapter 2

pp. 20–24: BM 1998,0901.22, 1998,0901.20, 1998,0901.33, 1998,0901.27, 1998,0901.28; WG.32, 1857,0627.1-13; 2002,0701.1-6
p. 25: Courtesy of the Cambridge Archaeological Unit, University of Cambridge
pp. 26–8: BM WG.1712-WG.1718, WG.1720, WG.1721; 1858,1115.1-5; 1911,1021.6, 1865,0207.1, 1911,1021.8, 1911,1021.15, WG.1276, WG.1321-4, WG.1343, WG.1337, WG.1340, WG.1282, WG.1272
p.30: Norwich Castle Museum and Art Gallery
pp. 31–9: BM 1998,0901.22, 1998,0901.20, 1998,0901.33, 1998,0901.27, 1998,0901.28; 2010,8032. (various); 2010,8032.7; 1998,0401.1-22; 1989,0601.21, 1989,0601.5, 1989,0601.6, 1989,0601.12, 1989,0601.20,

1989,0601.37, 1989,0601.88, 1989,0601.162, 1989,0601.186, 1989,0601.190, 1989,0601.200, 1989,0601.278; 1846,0322.112-3, 1846,0322,143, 1889,0706.78, 1889,0706.79, 1846,0322.108, 1889,0706.77, 1846,0322.96, 1846,0322.68; 1847,0208.82, 1847,0208.48, 1847,0208.31, 1847,0208.51, 1847,0208.55, 1847,0208.77, 1847,0208.84, 1847,0208.83, 1847,0208.41
p. 40: BM 2007,8034
pp. 41–3: 1991,0501.120, 1991,0501.121-124, 1991,0702.10-12, 1991,0501.1-5, 1991,0501.130-1, 1991,0501.118, 1991,0904.5; 2001,0901.1-9; 1982,0601.1-3
p. 45: Norfolk Museums TBC
p. 46: BM 1927,1207.1 (flint), 1927,1011.1-7 and 1927,1013.1-7 (coins)
p. 47: Harborough Museum, Leicestershire. Photo © the Trustees of the British Museum

Chapter 3

pp. 48–54: BM1925,0610.1-4, 1925,0610.7-9; 1817,0308.3-4; R.7561; 2013,4101.1-15; Coins 1912,0607.49-208 Pot n/a
p. 55: Photo: akg-images / Peter Connolly
pp. 56–60: BM1814,0705.1; 1814,0705.1-35
p. 61: Courtesy of the Portable Antiquities Scheme
pp. 62–3: the Roman Baths, Bath. Photos © the Trustees of the British Museum
pp. 64–5: BM 1928,1020.1 spoon, 1928,1019.1 pot, 1928,1101.1-41 coins; 1897,0913.1
p.66: Image courtesy of York Museums Trust
p. 67: BM 2013,4049.1-201, 2013,8011.1-2
p. 68: Photo © the Trustees of the British Museum
p. 69: South West Heritage Trust and Somerset Archaeological and Natural History Society
p. 70: BM1986,0401.1-356
p. 71: From the collections of Bucks County Museum. Photo: Saul Peckham, The Trustees of the British Museum, London

pp. 72–7: BM1946,1007.1-34; 1981,0201.1, 1981,0201.24-40; 1975,1002.10, 1975,1002.11; 1994,0408.36, 1994,0408.35, 1994,0408.34; 1994,0408.86-90, 1994,0408.81-85; 1994,0408.62-3;

Chapter 4

pp. 78–9: BM1855,0815.1-31
p. 81: Worthing Museum. Photo © the Trustees of the British Museum
pp. 82–6: BM 2003,0713.1-4; 1860,1024.2; 1939,1010.2.a-l; 1939,1003.41; 1994,0424.1-114
p. 87: © Ashmolean Museum, University of Oxford
p. 88 top: © Birmingham Museums Trust
p. 88 bottom: Courtesy of the Portable Antiquities Scheme
p. 89: Courtesy of the Portable Antiquities Scheme
pp. 90–97: BM 1838,0710 and 1841,0711 and others; 1944,0401.56; 2009,8023.1-76; AF.541; 1991,0109.1-8; 1912,0723.1-17

Chapter 5

pp. 98–100: BM 1967,1208.1-5; 7-9; 1994,0719.53
p. 102: photo © The Trustees of the British Museum, reproduced with kind permission of the Colchester and Ipswich Museum Service
p. 104: BM E.2347 and various
p. 105: From Mosley, O. 1832. *History of the Castle, Priory and Town of Tutbury, In the County of Stafford*, London: Longman.
pp. 106–9: BM1967,1208.8; 1967,1208.7; 1914,0423.6-17; 1914,0423.19-20
p. 110: Courtesy of the Portable Antiquities Scheme
p. 111: Image courtesy of York Museums Trust
pp. 112–13: BM E.5089, 1956,1010.7, E.4343, 1935,0401.7732; 1907,0312.10-16
p. 114: Bank of England. Photo © The Trustees of the British Museum
p. 115: Courtesy of the Portable Antiquities Scheme and the Museum of London
p120: Courtesy of the Portable Antiquities Scheme

Index